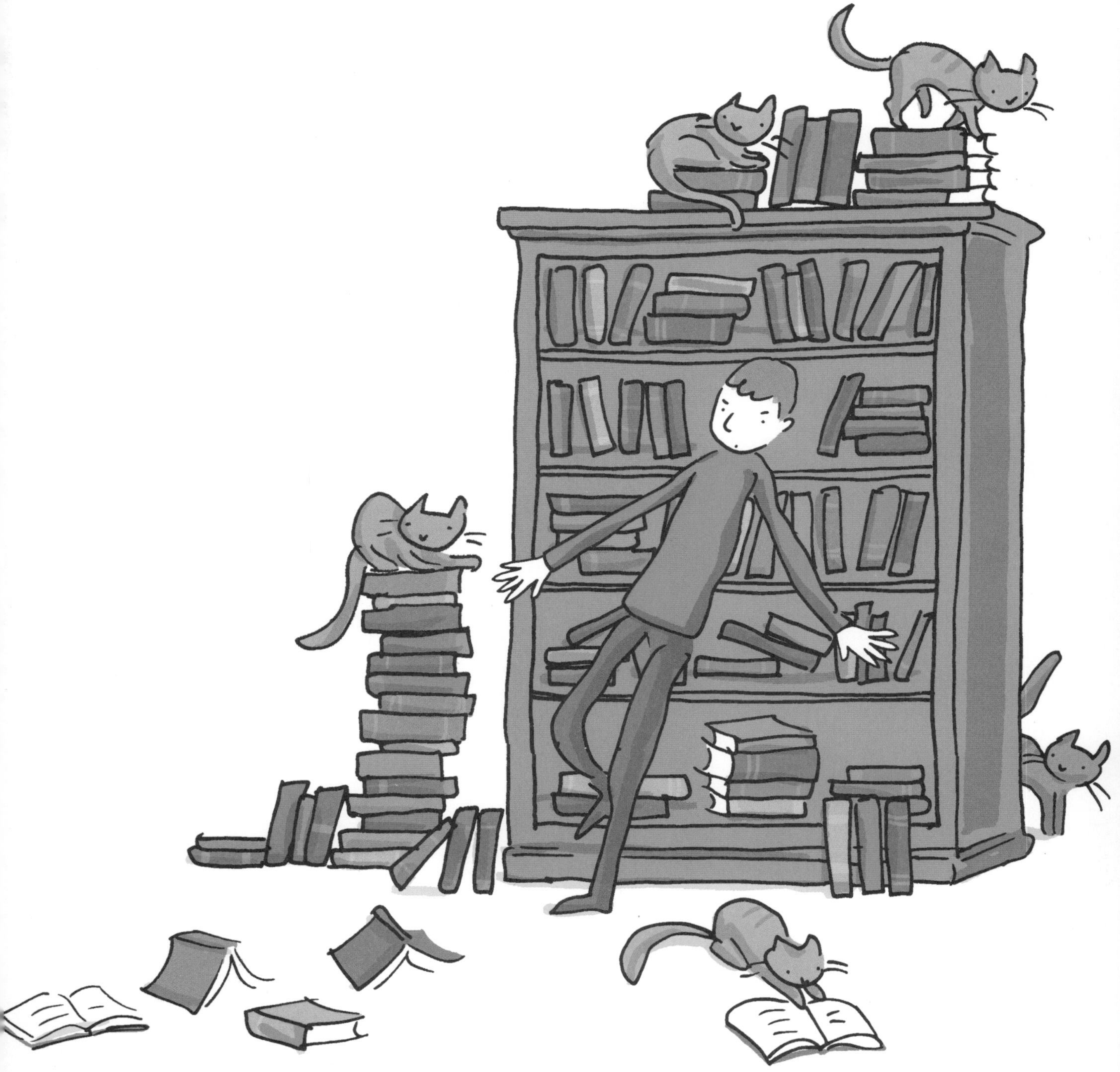

To my parents, for always letting me steal
from their bookshelf.

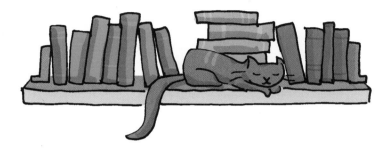

Thanks to my first reader, Kayla, for everything. Without you I would waste all my time eating bowls of Lucky Charms while obsessing over color variations in Photoshop. Thanks to my second reader and second brain, Gavin. Thanks to Charlie Kochman and Judy Hansen for making this book a reality. Thanks to Pam Notarantonio and Theresa Venezia for their design expertise and putting up with my unconventional formatting. Thanks to Pamela Paul, Nicholas Blechman, Matt Dorfman, Lauren Christensen, Parul Sehgal, Gal Beckerman, and everyone else at the *New York Times Book Review*—the back page has been a wonderful canvas for my ideas. Thanks to Lou Ann Walker and the rest of the *Southampton Review* for publishing my comics in the same pages as Billy Collins. Thanks to everyone at the *Kansas City Star* for taking an early chance on my comics and letting me misspell onomatopoeia in every possible way. Thanks to all my cartooning heroes—if you look closely, you can see their influence in every line. And thanks to all the librarians at the Wichita Public Library and Derby Public Library who continue to let me check out ridiculous amounts of books with very little hassle.

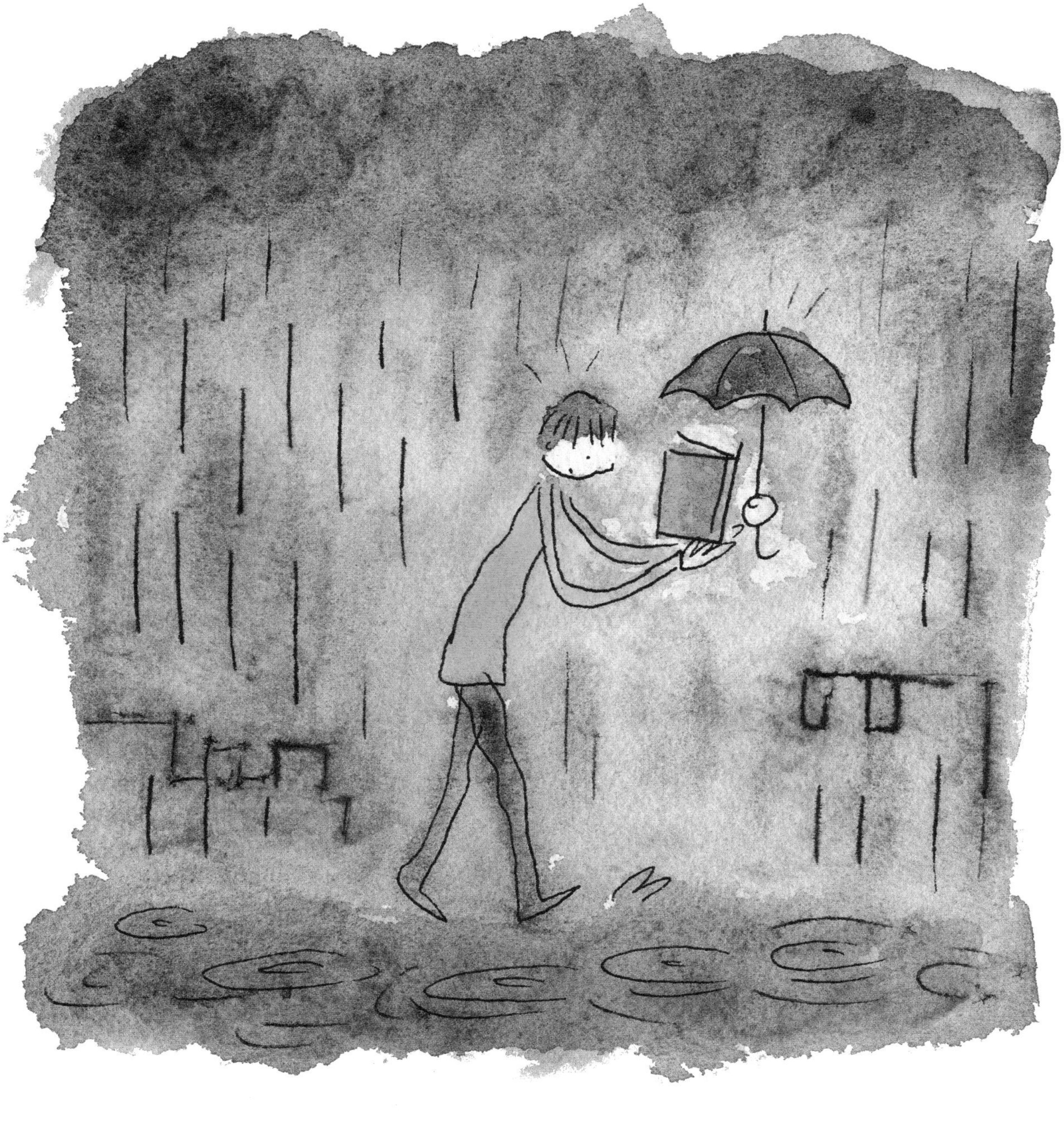

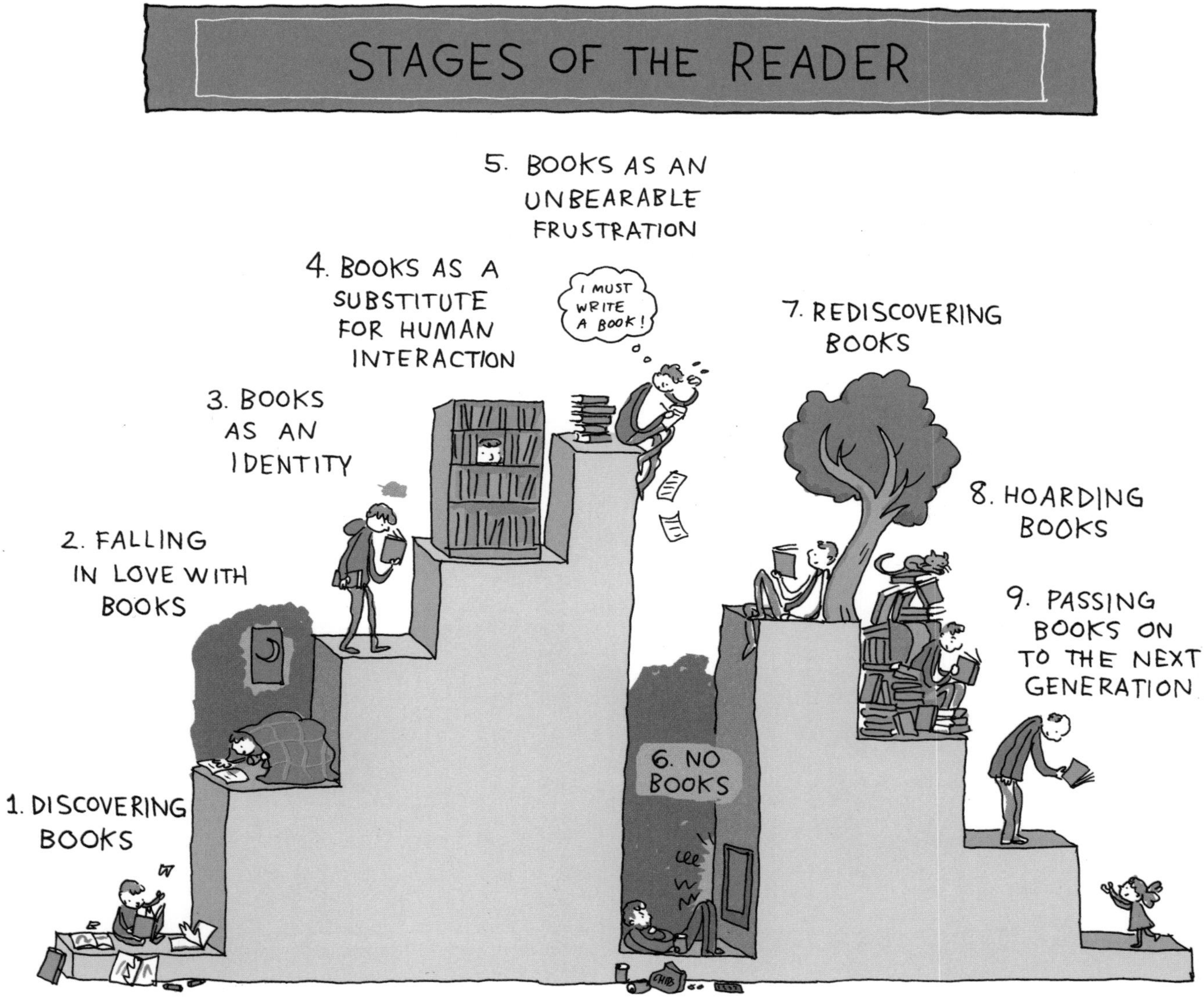
STAGES OF THE READER
1. DISCOVERING BOOKS
2. FALLING IN LOVE WITH BOOKS
3. BOOKS AS AN IDENTITY
4. BOOKS AS A SUBSTITUTE FOR HUMAN INTERACTION
5. BOOKS AS AN UNBEARABLE FRUSTRATION
I MUST WRITE A BOOK!
6. NO BOOKS
7. REDISCOVERING BOOKS
8. HOARDING BOOKS
9. PASSING BOOKS ON TO THE NEXT GENERATION

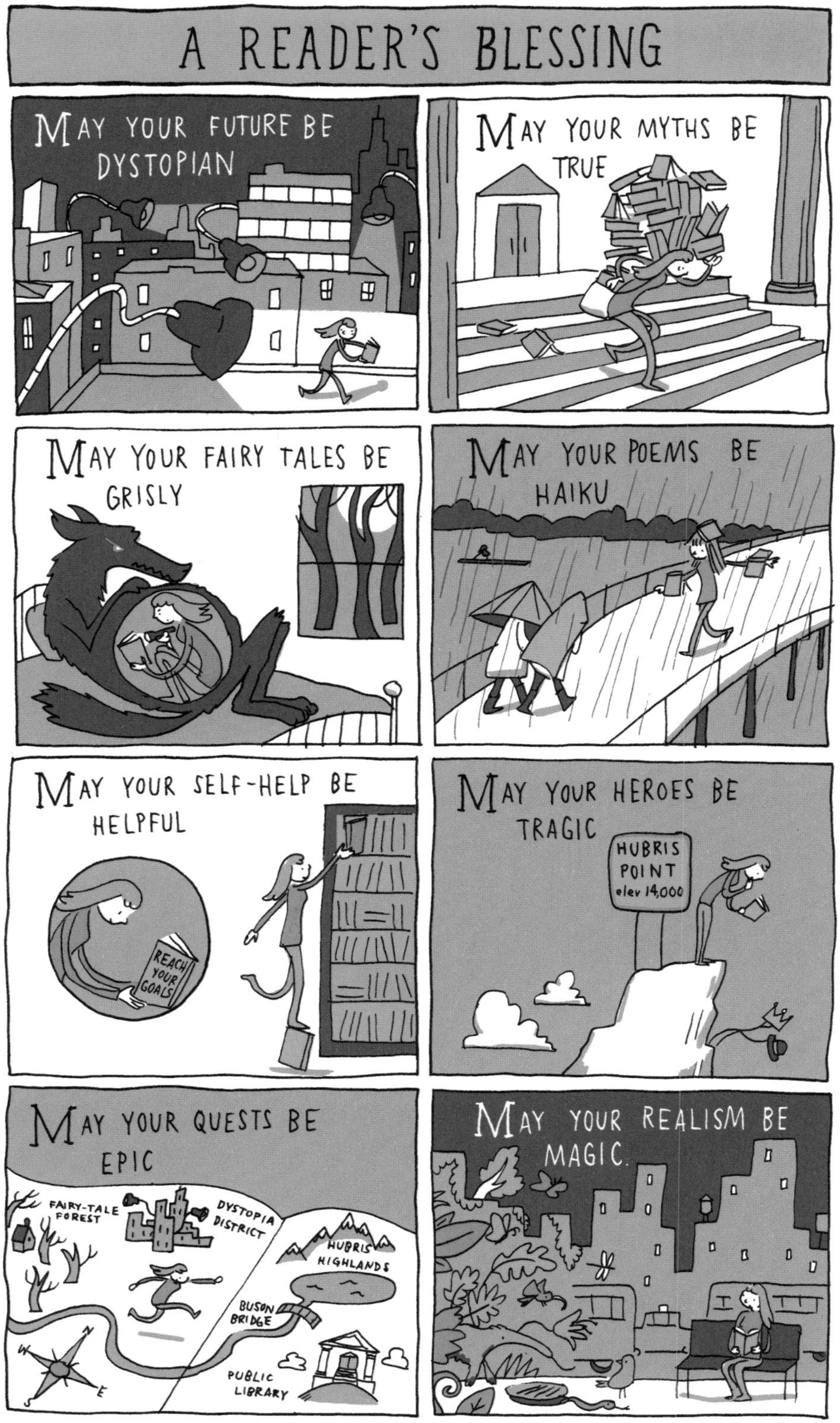
A READER'S BLESSING
MAY YOUR FUTURE BE DYSTOPIAN
MAY YOUR MYTHS BE TRUE
MAY YOUR FAIRY TALES BE GRISLY
MAY YOUR POEMS BE HAIKU
MAY YOUR SELF-HELP BE HELPFUL
REACH YOUR GOALS
MAY YOUR HEROES BE TRAGIC
HUBRIS POINT elev 14,000
MAY YOUR QUESTS BE EPIC
FAIRY-TALE FOREST
DYSTOPIA DISTRICT
HUBRIS HIGHLANDS
BUSON BRIDGE
PUBLIC LIBRARY
MAY YOUR REALISM BE MAGIC.

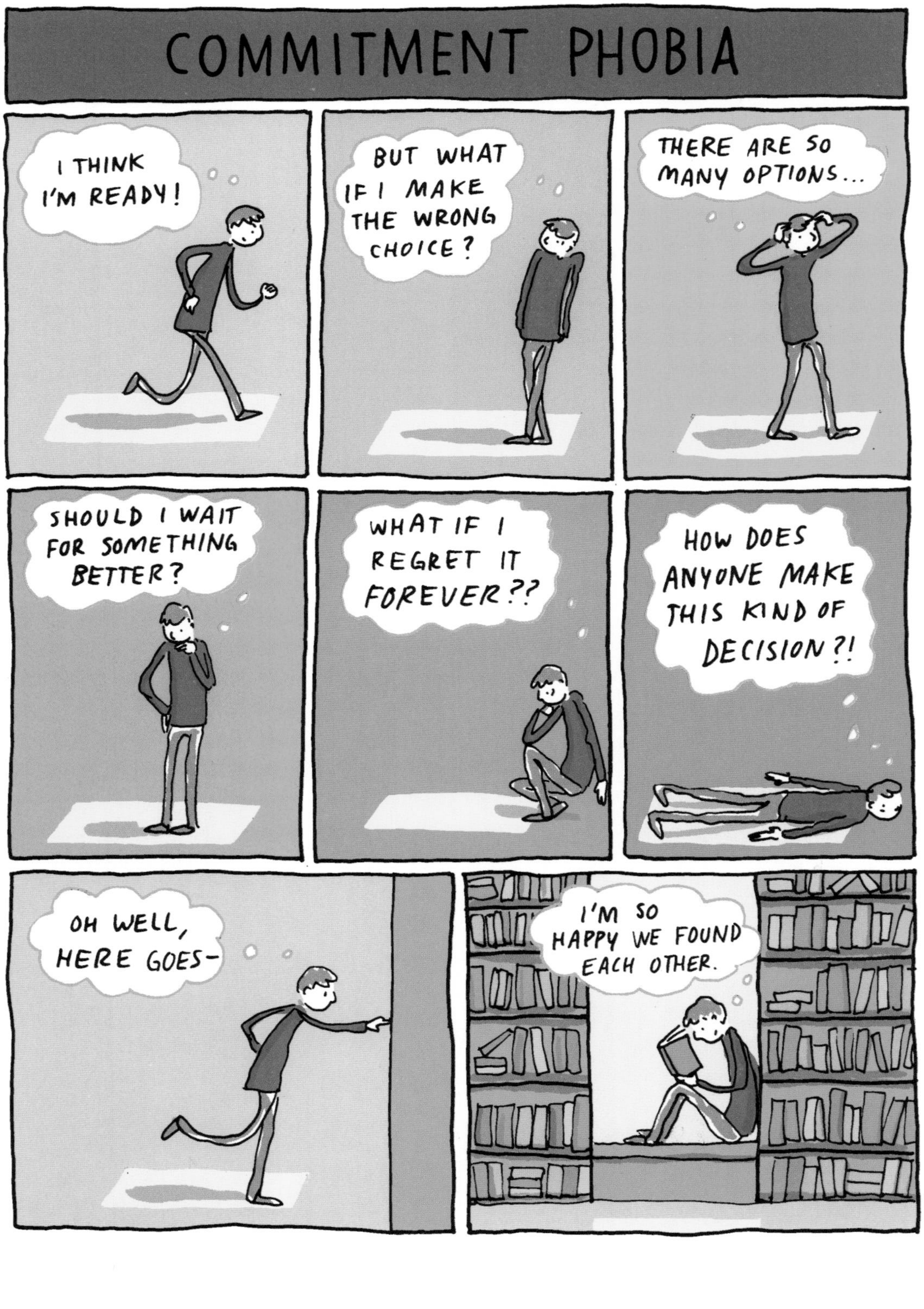
COMMITMENT PHOBIA
I THINK I'M READY!
BUT WHAT IF I MAKE THE WRONG CHOICE?
THERE ARE SO MANY OPTIONS...
SHOULD I WAIT FOR SOMETHING BETTER?
WHAT IF I REGRET IT FOREVER??
HOW DOES ANYONE MAKE THIS KIND OF DECISION?!
OH WELL, HERE GOES-
I'M SO HAPPY WE FOUND EACH OTHER.

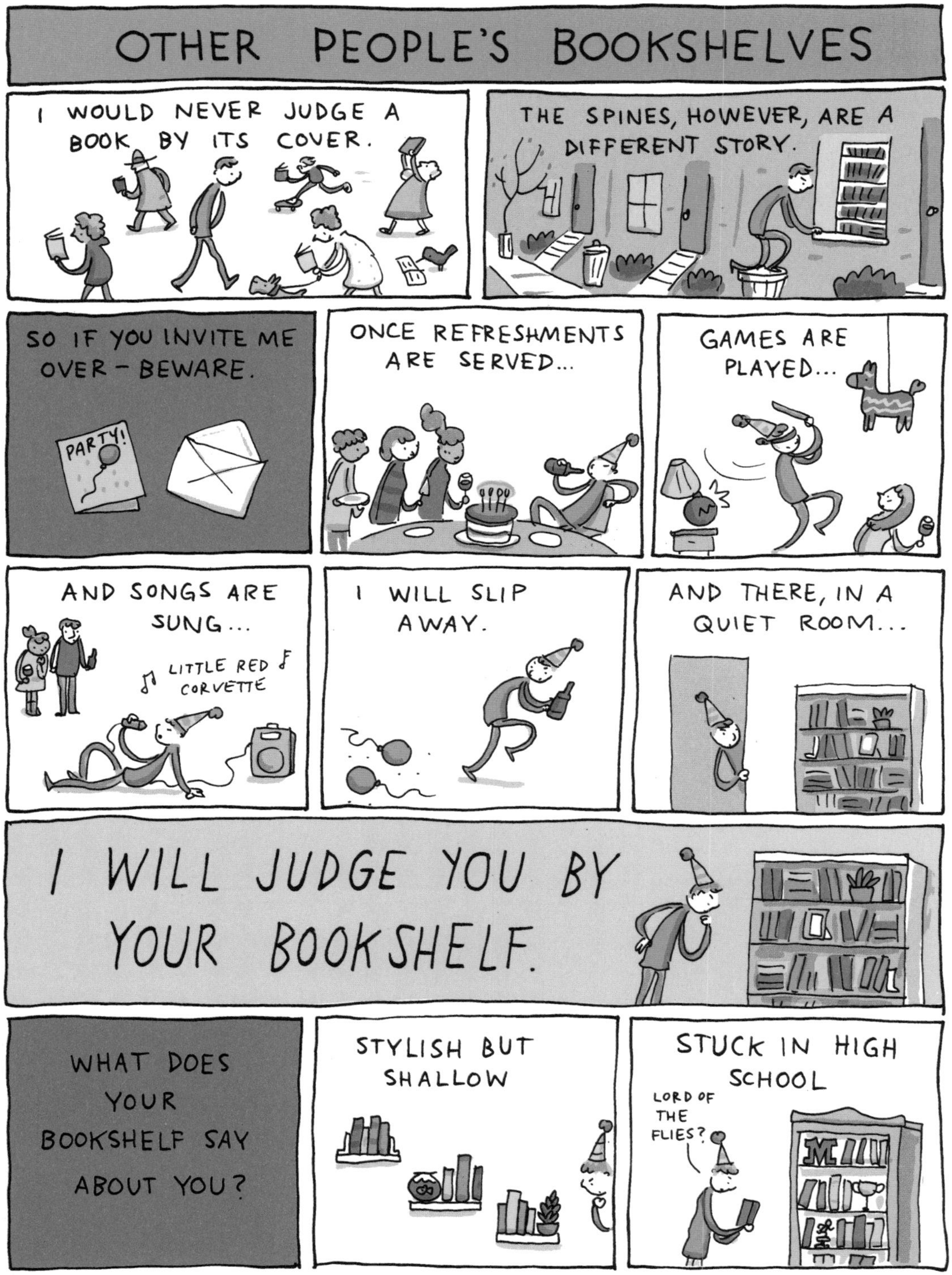
OTHER PEOPLE'S BOOKSHELVES
I WOULD NEVER JUDGE A BOOK BY ITS COVER.
THE SPINES, HOWEVER, ARE A DIFFERENT STORY.
SO IF YOU INVITE ME OVER – BEWARE.
PARTY!
ONCE REFRESHMENTS ARE SERVED...
GAMES ARE PLAYED...
AND SONGS ARE SUNG...
LITTLE RED CORVETTE
I WILL SLIP AWAY.
AND THERE, IN A QUIET ROOM...
I WILL JUDGE YOU BY YOUR BOOKSHELF.
WHAT DOES YOUR BOOKSHELF SAY ABOUT YOU?
STYLISH BUT SHALLOW
STUCK IN HIGH SCHOOL
LORD OF THE FLIES?

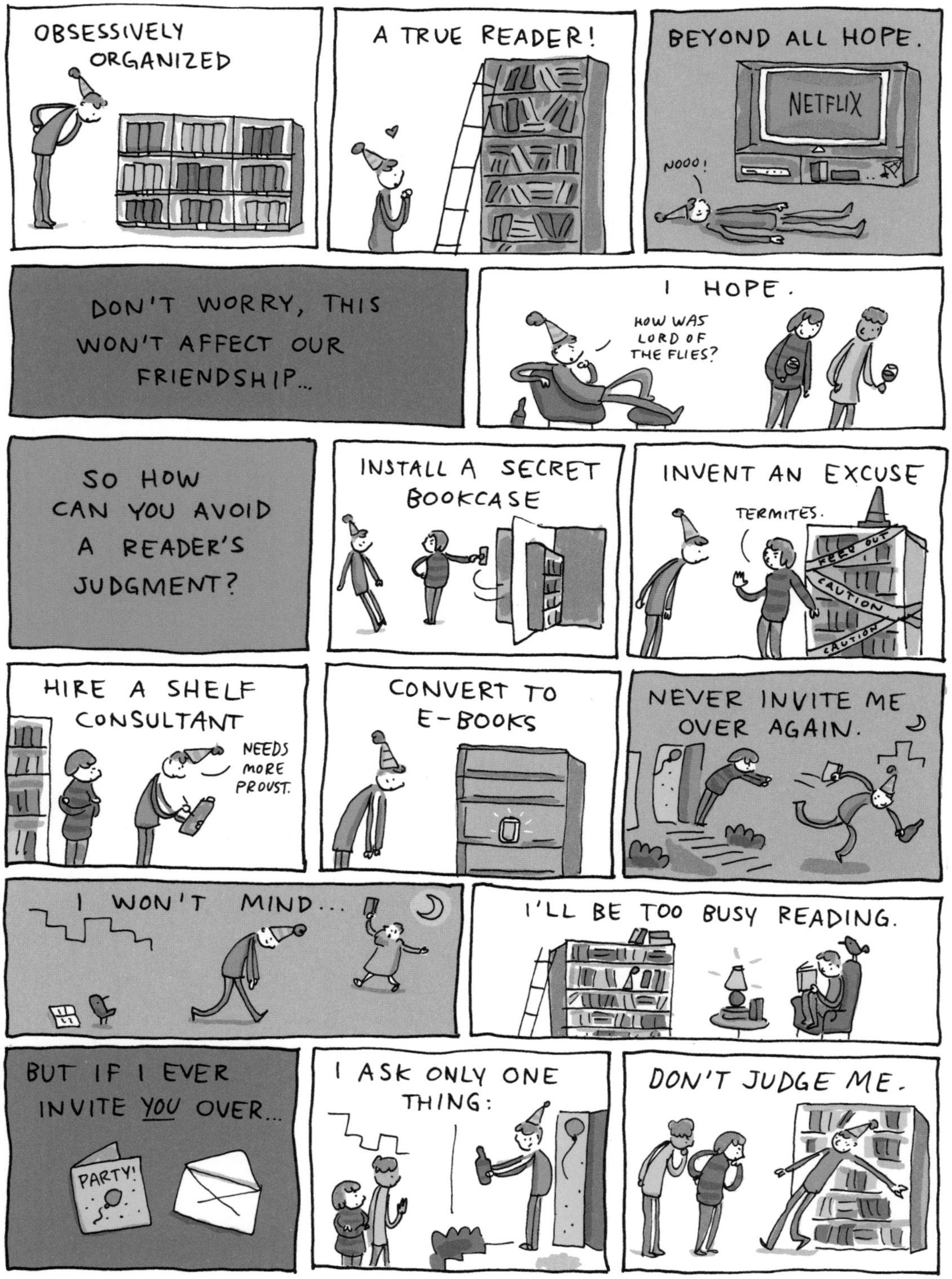
OBSESSIVELY ORGANIZED
A TRUE READER!
BEYOND ALL HOPE.
NETFLIX
NOOO!
DON'T WORRY, THIS WON'T AFFECT OUR FRIENDSHIP...
I HOPE.
HOW WAS LORD OF THE FLIES?
SO HOW CAN YOU AVOID A READER'S JUDGMENT?
INSTALL A SECRET BOOKCASE
INVENT AN EXCUSE
TERMITES.
KEEP OUT
CAUTION
CAUTION
HIRE A SHELF CONSULTANT
NEEDS MORE PROUST.
CONVERT TO E-BOOKS
NEVER INVITE ME OVER AGAIN.
I WON'T MIND...
I'LL BE TOO BUSY READING.
BUT IF I EVER INVITE YOU OVER...
PARTY!
I ASK ONLY ONE THING:
DON'T JUDGE ME.

I read
in social
situations.

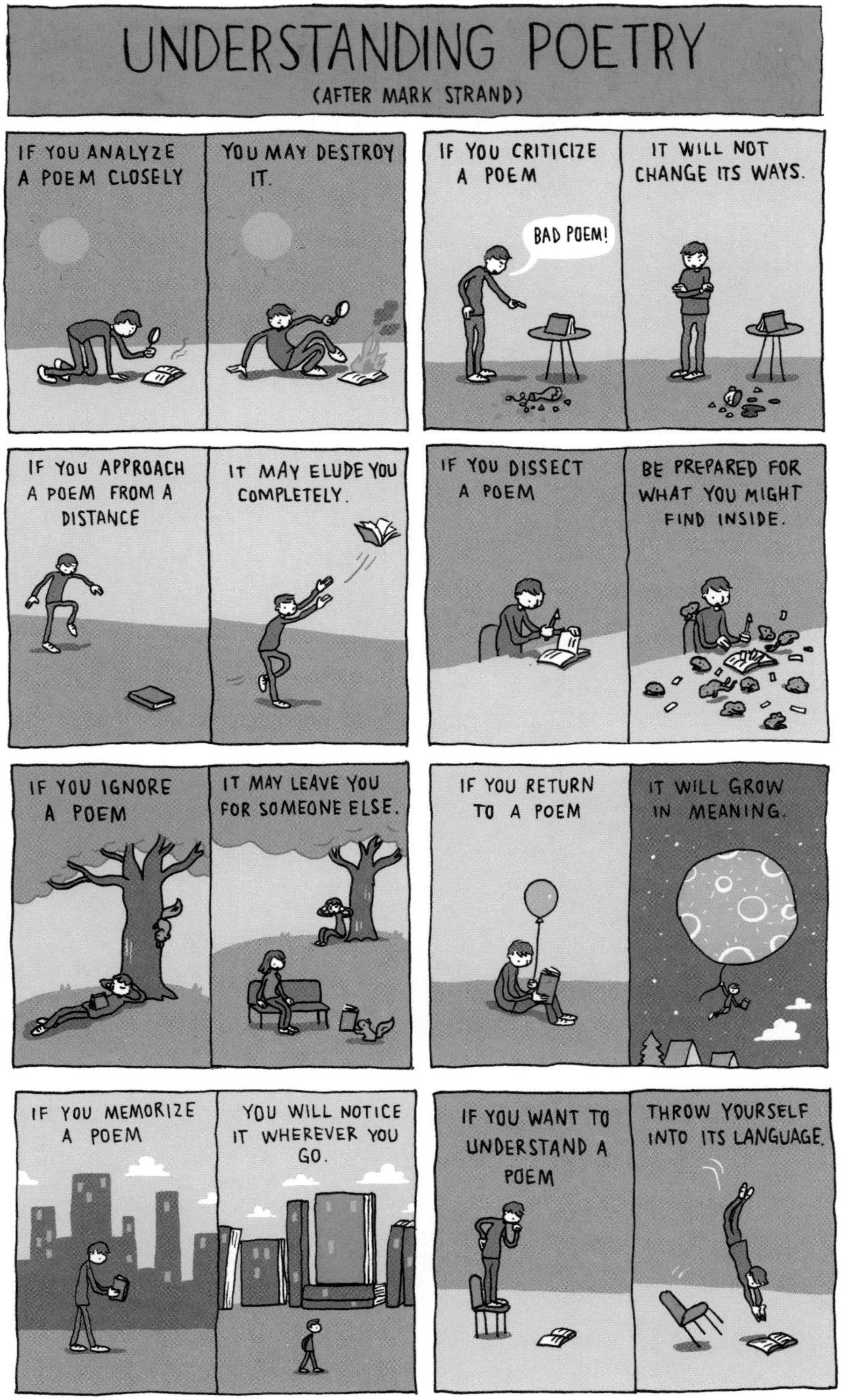
UNDERSTANDING POETRY
(AFTER MARK STRAND)
IF YOU ANALYZE A POEM CLOSELY
YOU MAY DESTROY IT.
IF YOU CRITICIZE A POEM
BAD POEM!
IT WILL NOT CHANGE ITS WAYS.
IF YOU APPROACH A POEM FROM A DISTANCE
IT MAY ELUDE YOU COMPLETELY.
IF YOU DISSECT A POEM
BE PREPARED FOR WHAT YOU MIGHT FIND INSIDE.
IF YOU IGNORE A POEM
IT MAY LEAVE YOU FOR SOMEONE ELSE.
IF YOU RETURN TO A POEM
IT WILL GROW IN MEANING.
IF YOU MEMORIZE A POEM
YOU WILL NOTICE IT WHEREVER YOU GO.
IF YOU WANT TO UNDERSTAND A POEM
THROW YOURSELF INTO ITS LANGUAGE.

ODE TO AN UNFINISHED BOOK

I ADMIT, I PICKED YOU UP WITH UNREALISTIC EXPECTATIONS...

THE WAY I'D LOOK READING YOU THROUGH A COFFEE SHOP WINDOW.

THE HOURS I'D SPEND POOLSIDE, LOST IN YOUR WORLD.

HOW SMART I'D SOUND DISCUSSING YOU AT PARTIES.

BUT NOW HERE WE SIT.

YOU ON THE END TABLE.

ME IN MY CHAIR.

STUCK.

I TRY TO REASON THROUGH MY DILEMMA.

TO FINISH	NOT TO FINISH
- see how it ends	- more free time
- no READER'S GUILT	- can start a new book!
- build "GRIT"	- it's not for a grade
- won't be haunted by it FOREVER	- who am I trying to impress?

IT DEVOLVES INTO A POINTLESS PHILOSOPHICAL DEBATE.

IS THE BOOK HALF-FINISHED?

IS THE BOOK HALF-STARTED?

IS IT A SYMBOL OF MY INABILITY TO FINISH ANYTHING?

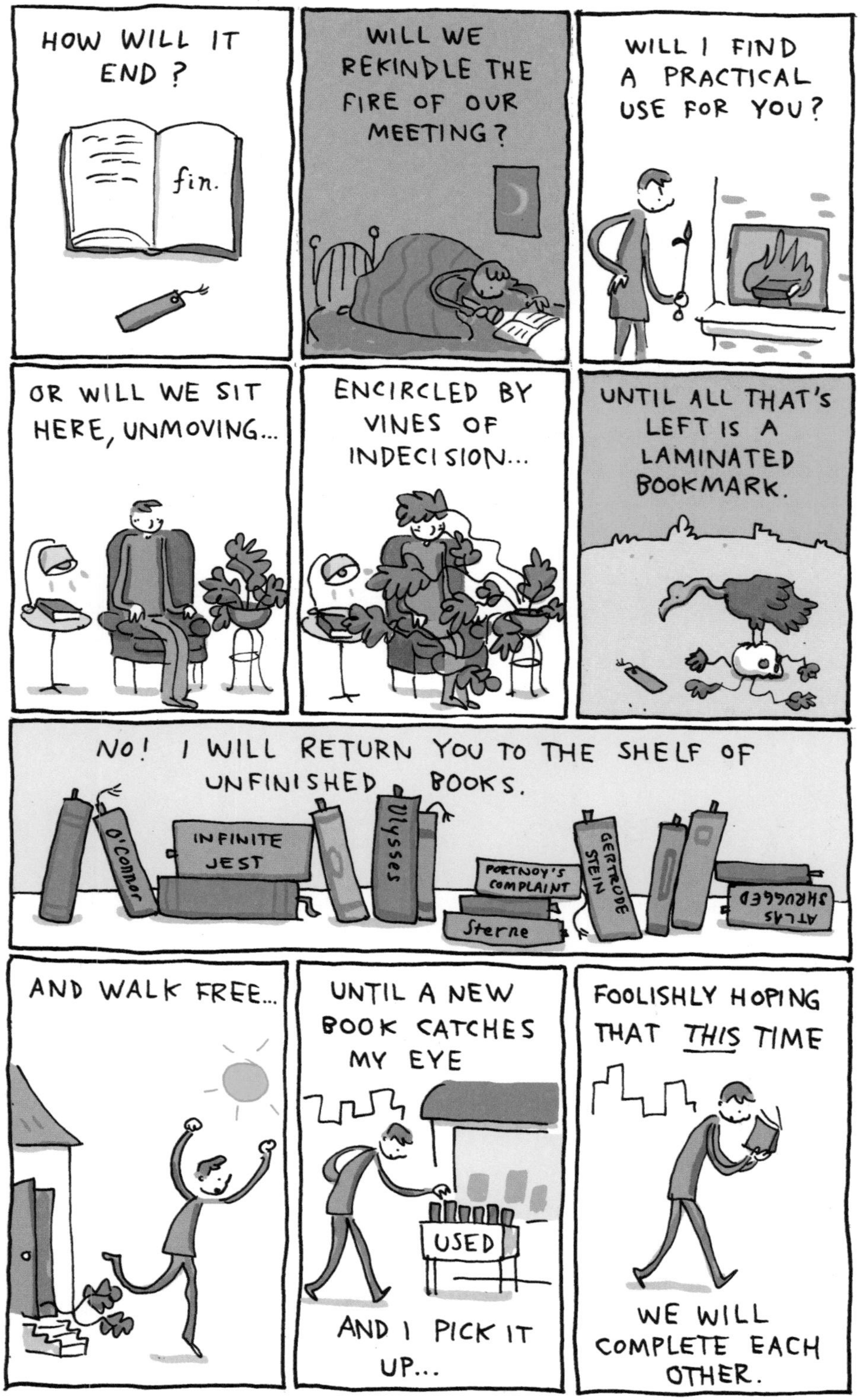
HOW WILL IT END?
fin.
WILL WE REKINDLE THE FIRE OF OUR MEETING?
WILL I FIND A PRACTICAL USE FOR YOU?
OR WILL WE SIT HERE, UNMOVING...
ENCIRCLED BY VINES OF INDECISION...
UNTIL ALL THAT'S LEFT IS A LAMINATED BOOKMARK.
NO! I WILL RETURN YOU TO THE SHELF OF UNFINISHED BOOKS.
O'Connor
INFINITE JEST
Ulysses
PORTNOY'S COMPLAINT
Sterne
GERTRUDE STEIN
ATLAS SHRUGGED
AND WALK FREE...
UNTIL A NEW BOOK CATCHES MY EYE
USED
AND I PICK IT UP...
FOOLISHLY HOPING THAT THIS TIME
WE WILL COMPLETE EACH OTHER.

I confuse
fiction
with reality.

THE STORY COASTER

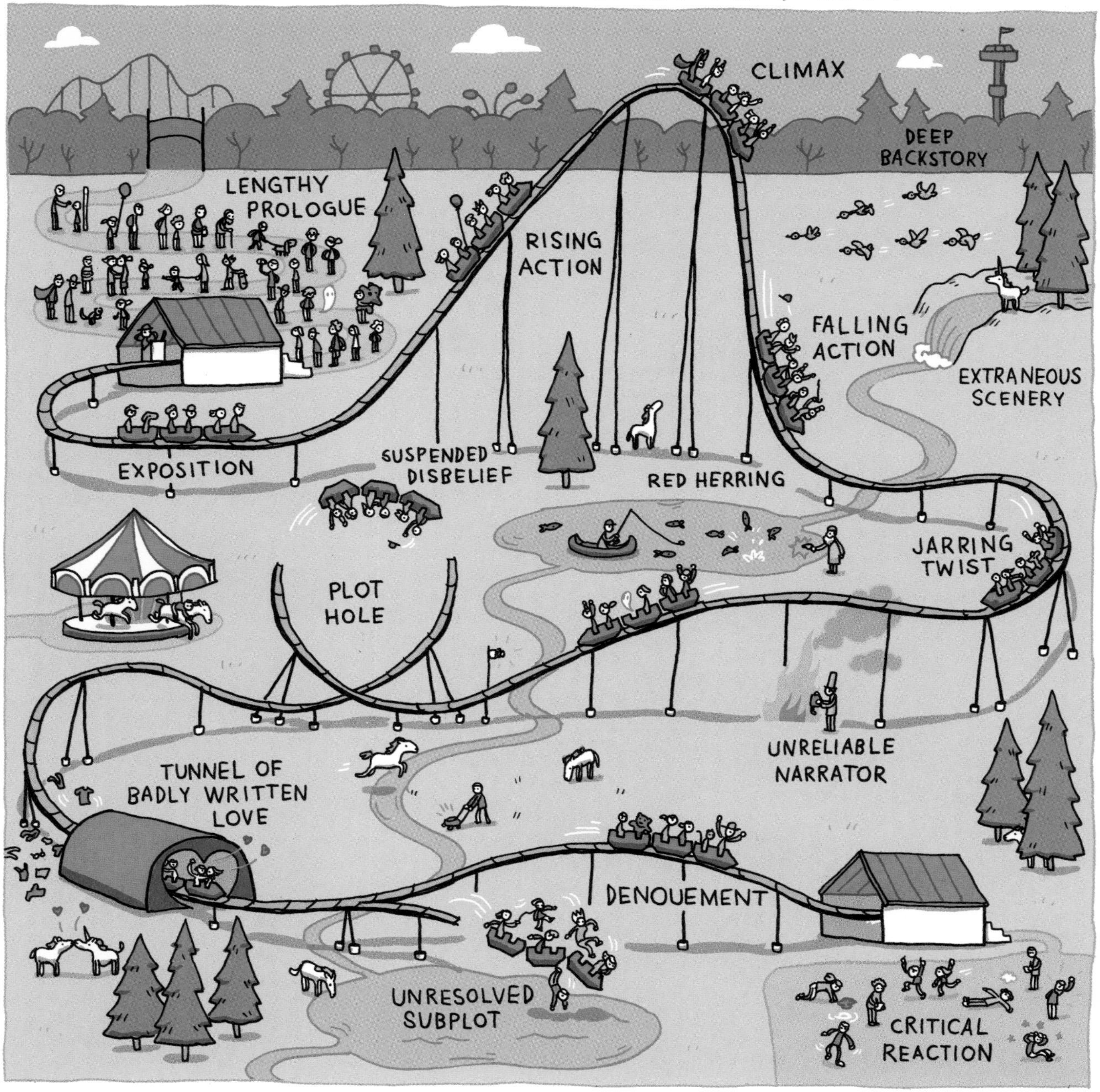
CLIMAX
DEEP BACKSTORY
LENGTHY PROLOGUE
RISING ACTION
FALLING ACTION
EXTRANEOUS SCENERY
EXPOSITION
SUSPENDED DISBELIEF
RED HERRING
JARRING TWIST
PLOT HOLE
UNRELIABLE NARRATOR
TUNNEL OF BADLY WRITTEN LOVE
DENOUEMENT
UNRESOLVED SUBPLOT
CRITICAL REACTION

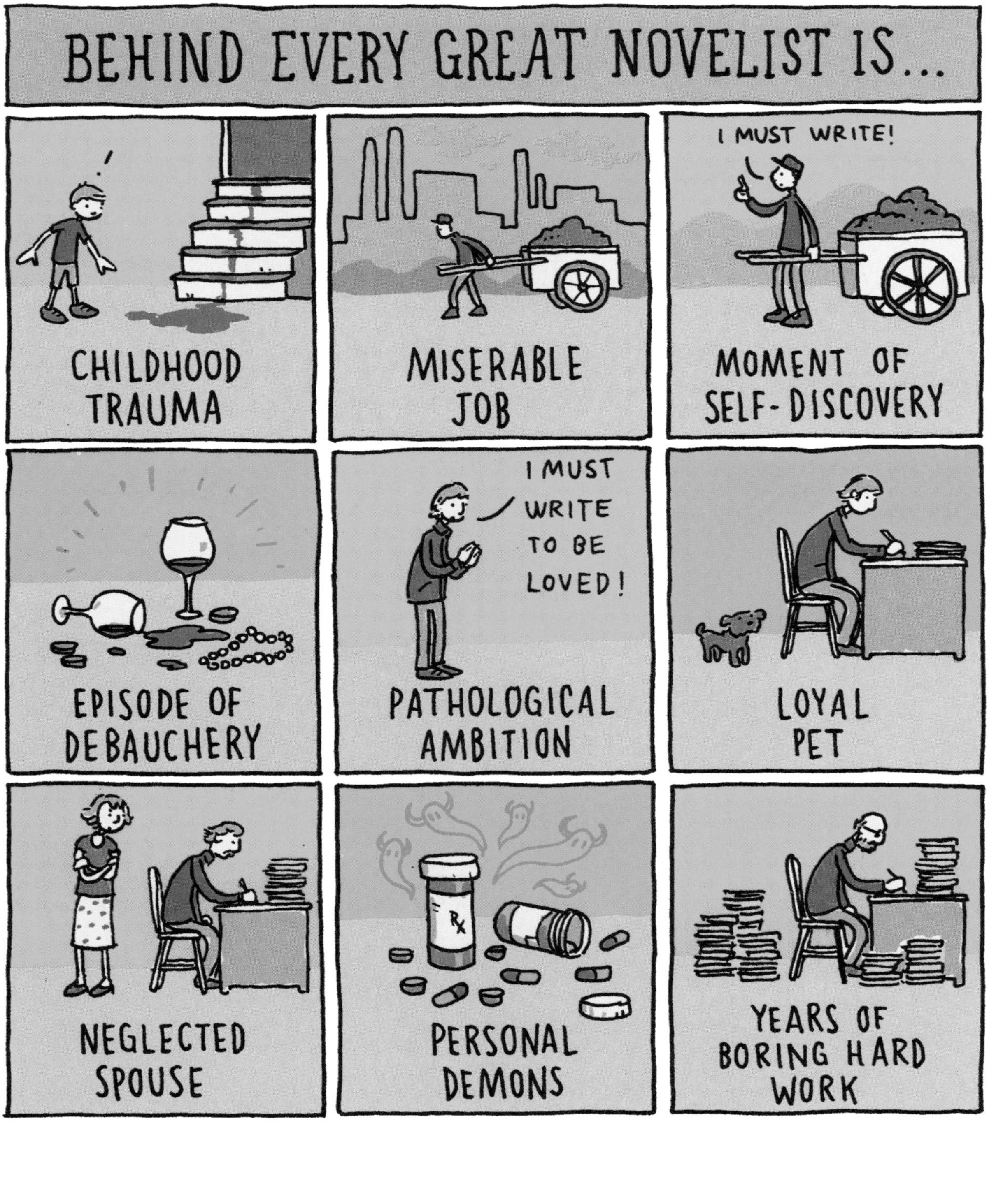
BEHIND EVERY GREAT NOVELIST IS...
!
CHILDHOOD TRAUMA
MISERABLE JOB
I MUST WRITE!
MOMENT OF SELF-DISCOVERY
EPISODE OF DEBAUCHERY
I MUST WRITE TO BE LOVED!
PATHOLOGICAL AMBITION
LOYAL PET
NEGLECTED SPOUSE
Rx
PERSONAL DEMONS
YEARS OF BORING HARD WORK

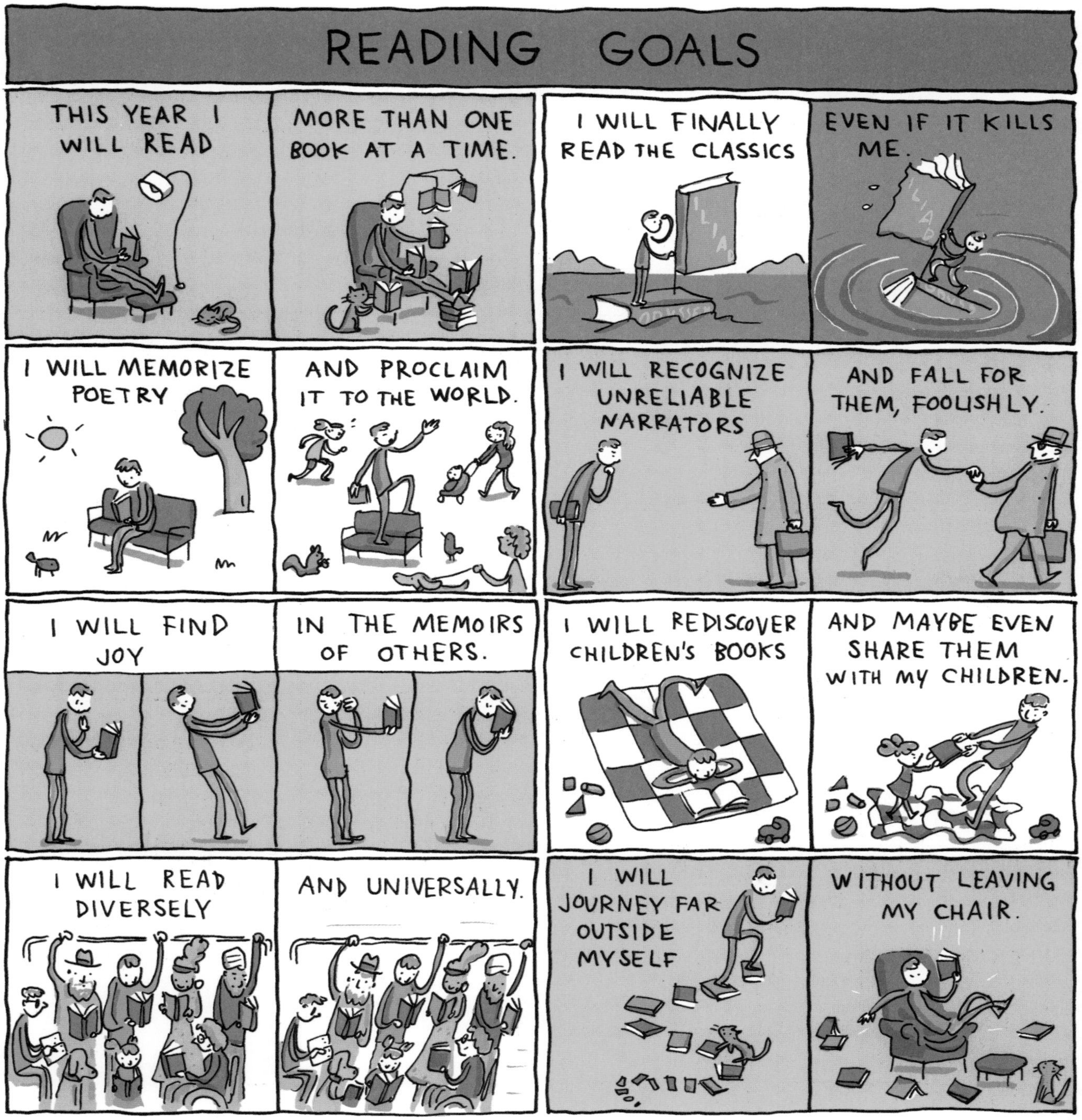
READING GOALS
THIS YEAR I WILL READ
MORE THAN ONE BOOK AT A TIME.
I WILL FINALLY READ THE CLASSICS
EVEN IF IT KILLS ME.
I WILL MEMORIZE POETRY
AND PROCLAIM IT TO THE WORLD.
I WILL RECOGNIZE UNRELIABLE NARRATORS
AND FALL FOR THEM, FOOLISHLY.
I WILL FIND JOY
IN THE MEMOIRS OF OTHERS.
I WILL REDISCOVER CHILDREN'S BOOKS
AND MAYBE EVEN SHARE THEM WITH MY CHILDREN.
I WILL READ DIVERSELY
AND UNIVERSALLY.
I WILL JOURNEY FAR OUTSIDE MYSELF
WITHOUT LEAVING MY CHAIR.

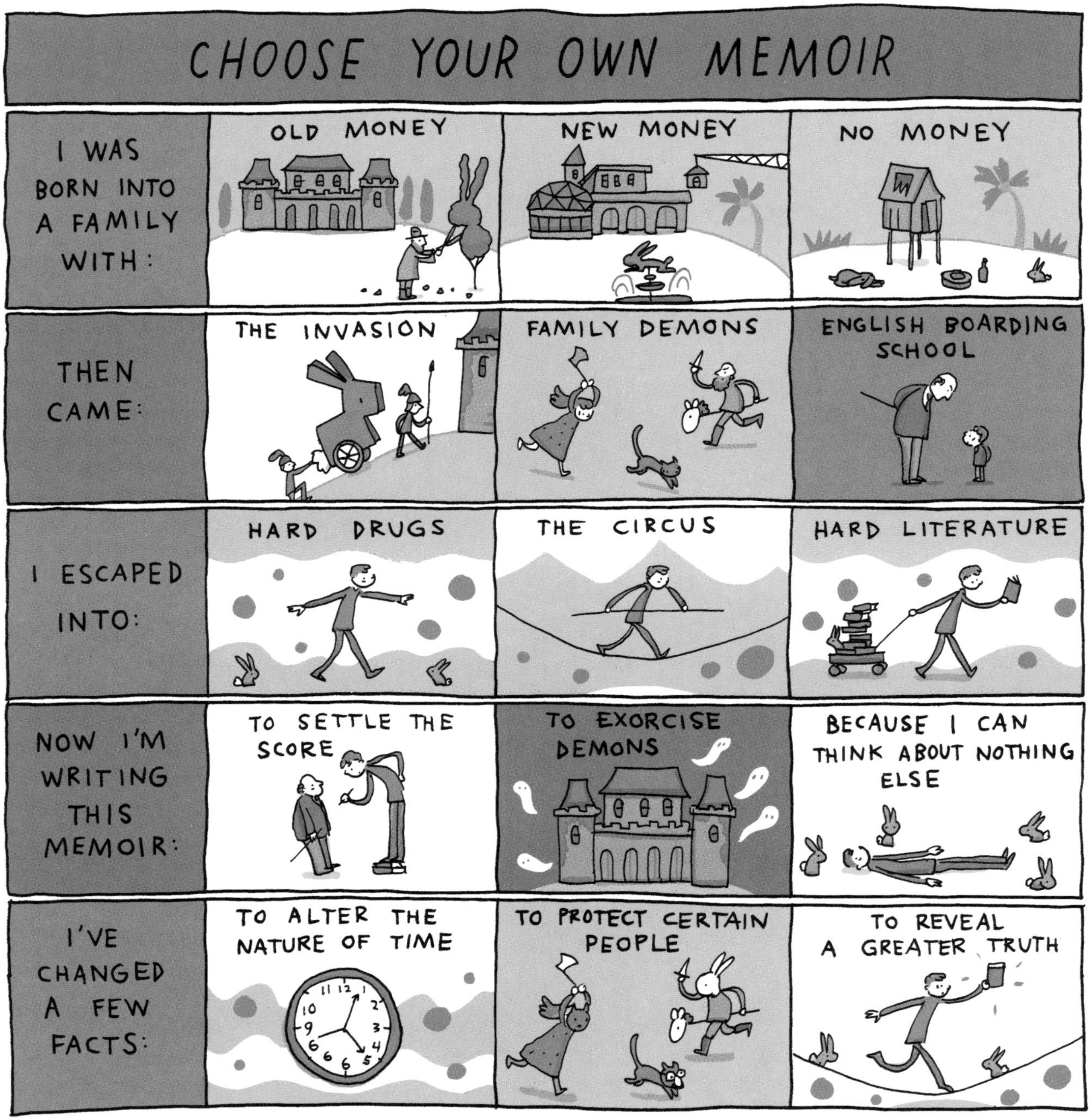
CHOOSE YOUR OWN MEMOIR
I WAS BORN INTO A FAMILY WITH:
OLD MONEY
NEW MONEY
NO MONEY
THEN CAME:
THE INVASION
FAMILY DEMONS
ENGLISH BOARDING SCHOOL
I ESCAPED INTO:
HARD DRUGS
THE CIRCUS
HARD LITERATURE
NOW I'M WRITING THIS MEMOIR:
TO SETTLE THE SCORE
TO EXORCISE DEMONS
BECAUSE I CAN THINK ABOUT NOTHING ELSE
I'VE CHANGED A FEW FACTS:
TO ALTER THE NATURE OF TIME
TO PROTECT CERTAIN PEOPLE
TO REVEAL A GREATER TRUTH

STORY LINES

(AFTER KURT VONNEGUT)

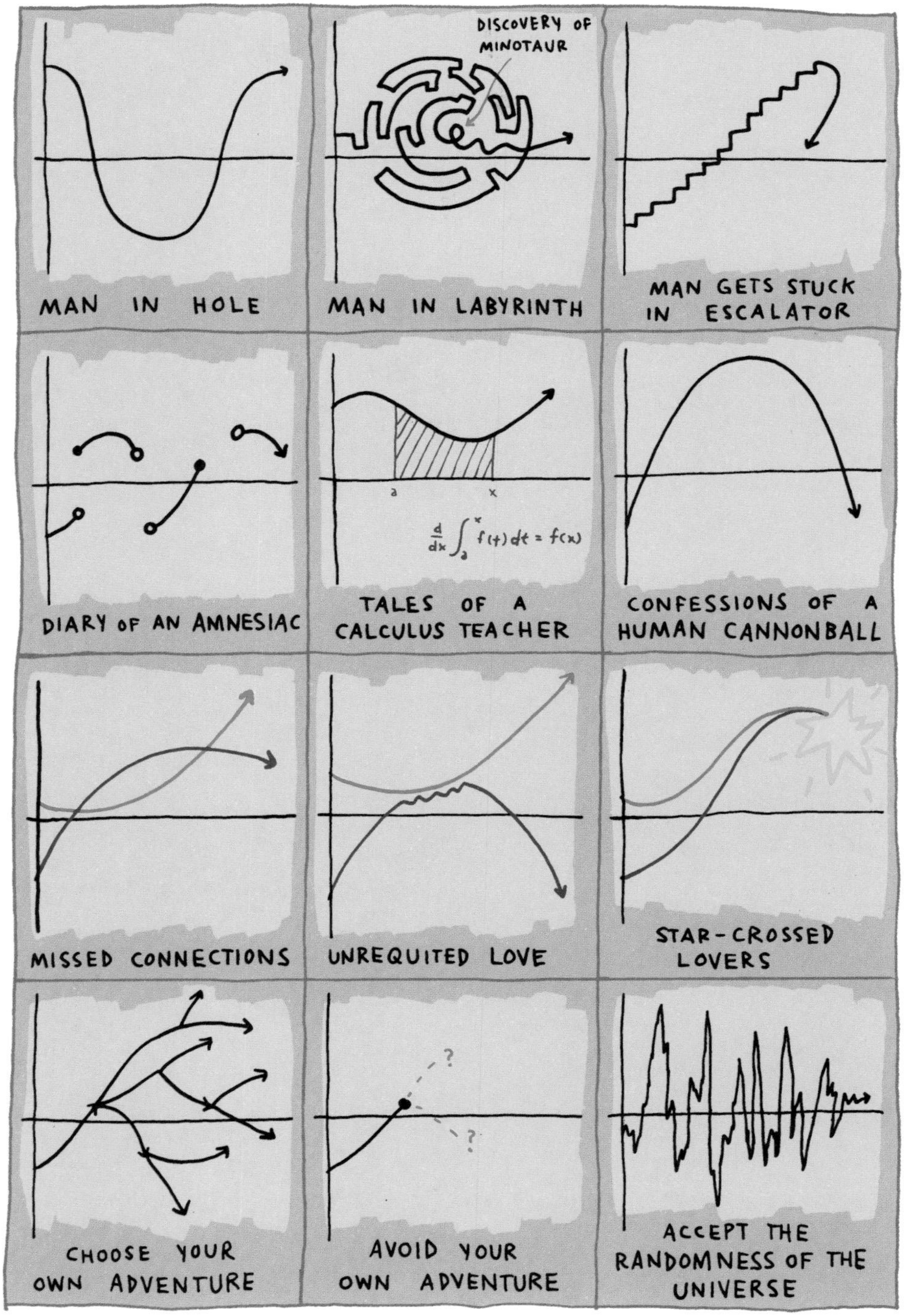
DISCOVERY OF MINOTAUR
MAN IN HOLE
MAN IN LABYRINTH
MAN GETS STUCK IN ESCALATOR
DIARY OF AN AMNESIAC
a
x
$\frac{d}{dx}\int_a^x f(t)\,dt = f(x)$
TALES OF A CALCULUS TEACHER
CONFESSIONS OF A HUMAN CANNONBALL
MISSED CONNECTIONS
UNREQUITED LOVE
STAR-CROSSED LOVERS
?
?
CHOOSE YOUR OWN ADVENTURE
AVOID YOUR OWN ADVENTURE
ACCEPT THE RANDOMNESS OF THE UNIVERSE

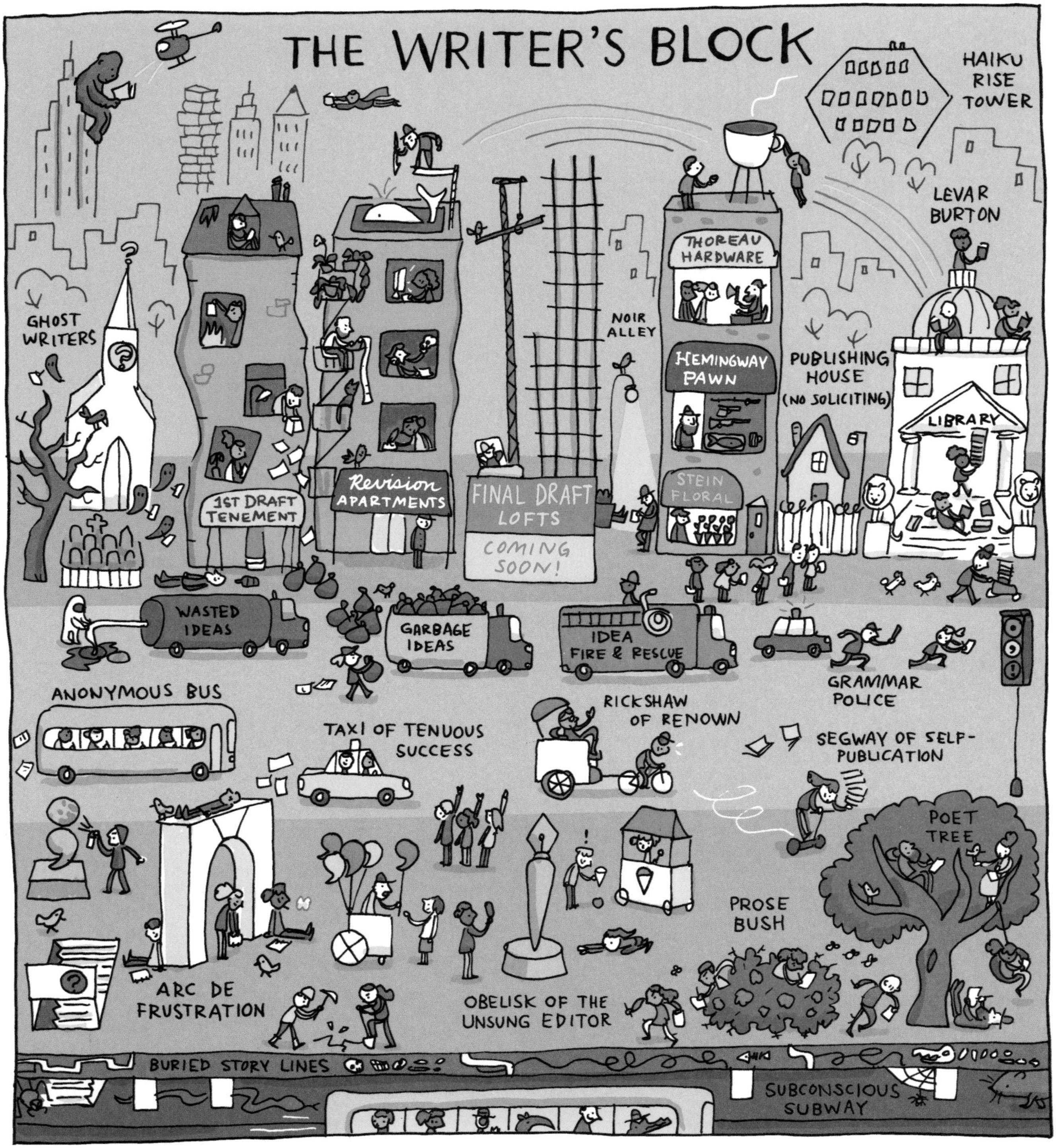
THE WRITER'S BLOCK
HAIKU RISE TOWER
LEVAR BURTON
GHOST WRITERS
1ST DRAFT TENEMENT
Revision APARTMENTS
FINAL DRAFT LOFTS
COMING SOON!
NOIR ALLEY
THOREAU HARDWARE
HEMINGWAY PAWN
STEIN FLORAL
PUBLISHING HOUSE (NO SOLICITING)
LIBRARY
WASTED IDEAS
GARBAGE IDEAS
IDEA FIRE & RESCUE
GRAMMAR POLICE
ANONYMOUS BUS
TAXI OF TENUOUS SUCCESS
RICKSHAW OF RENOWN
SEGWAY OF SELF-PUBLICATION
POET TREE
PROSE BUSH
ARC DE FRUSTRATION
OBELISK OF THE UNSUNG EDITOR
BURIED STORY LINES
SUBCONSCIOUS SUBWAY

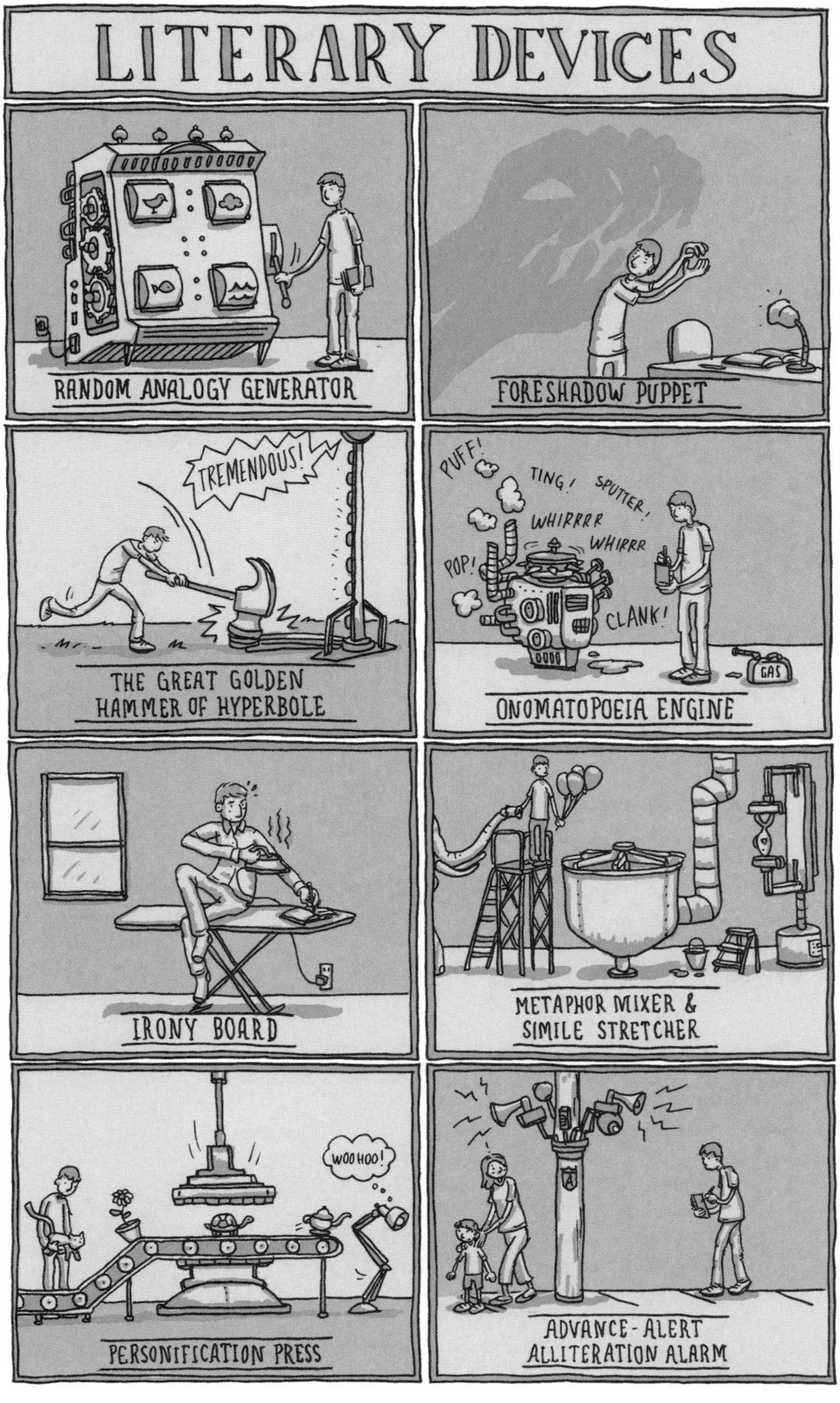
LITERARY DEVICES
RANDOM ANALOGY GENERATOR
FORESHADOW PUPPET
TREMENDOUS!
THE GREAT GOLDEN HAMMER OF HYPERBOLE
PUFF!
TING!
SPUTTER,
WHIRRRR
WHIRRR
POP!
CLANK!
GAS
ONOMATOPOEIA ENGINE
IRONY BOARD
METAPHOR MIXER & SIMILE STRETCHER
WOOHOO!
PERSONIFICATION PRESS
ADVANCE-ALERT ALLITERATION ALARM

I am
wanted for
unpaid library
fines.

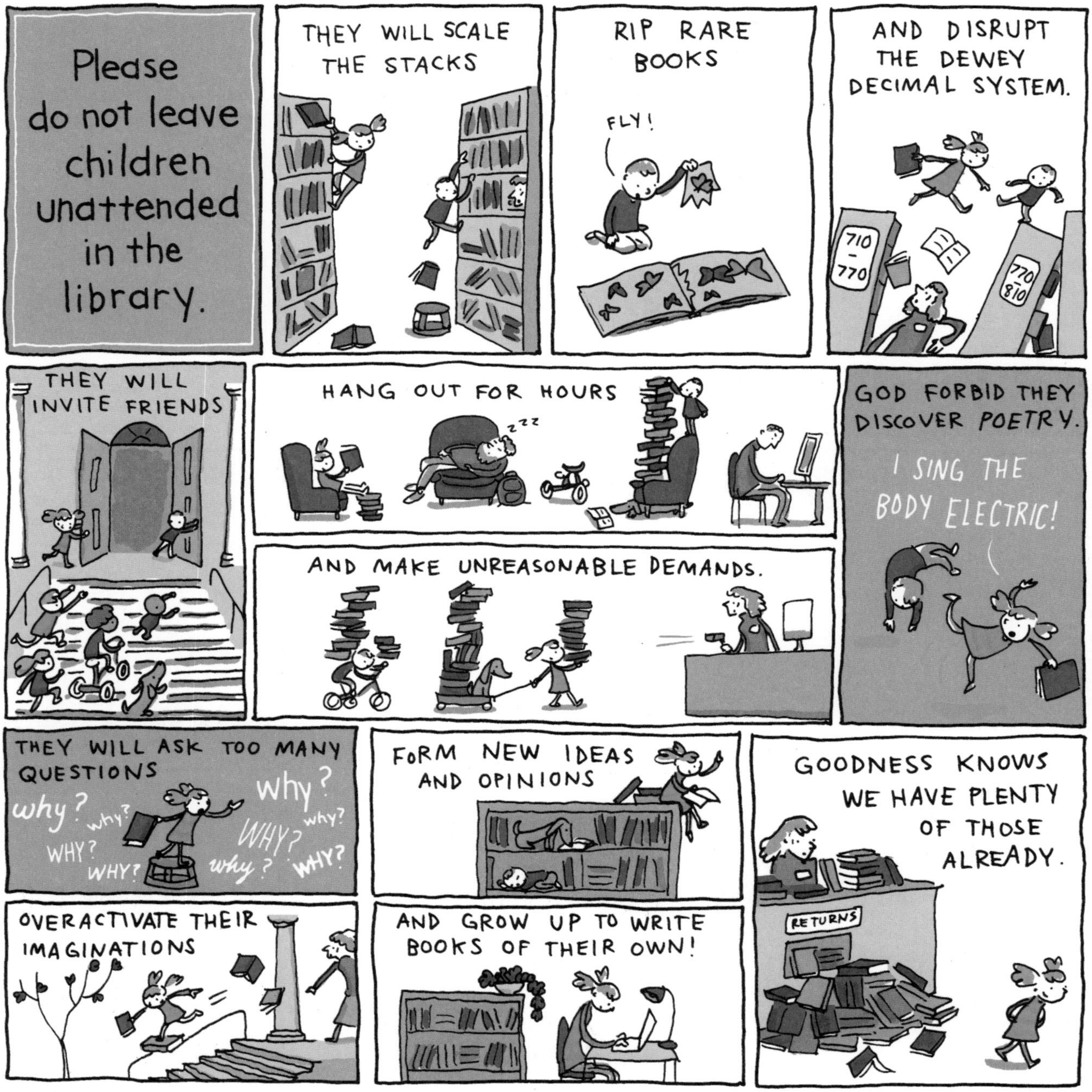
Please do not leave children unattended in the library.
THEY WILL SCALE THE STACKS
RIP RARE BOOKS
FLY!
AND DISRUPT THE DEWEY DECIMAL SYSTEM.
710 – 770
770 – 810
THEY WILL INVITE FRIENDS
HANG OUT FOR HOURS
ZZZ
AND MAKE UNREASONABLE DEMANDS.
GOD FORBID THEY DISCOVER *POETRY*.
I SING THE BODY ELECTRIC!
THEY WILL ASK TOO MANY QUESTIONS
why? why? WHY? WHY? why? WHY? why? why? WHY?
FORM NEW IDEAS AND OPINIONS
GOODNESS KNOWS WE HAVE PLENTY OF THOSE ALREADY.
RETURNS
OVERACTIVATE THEIR IMAGINATIONS
AND GROW UP TO WRITE BOOKS OF THEIR OWN!

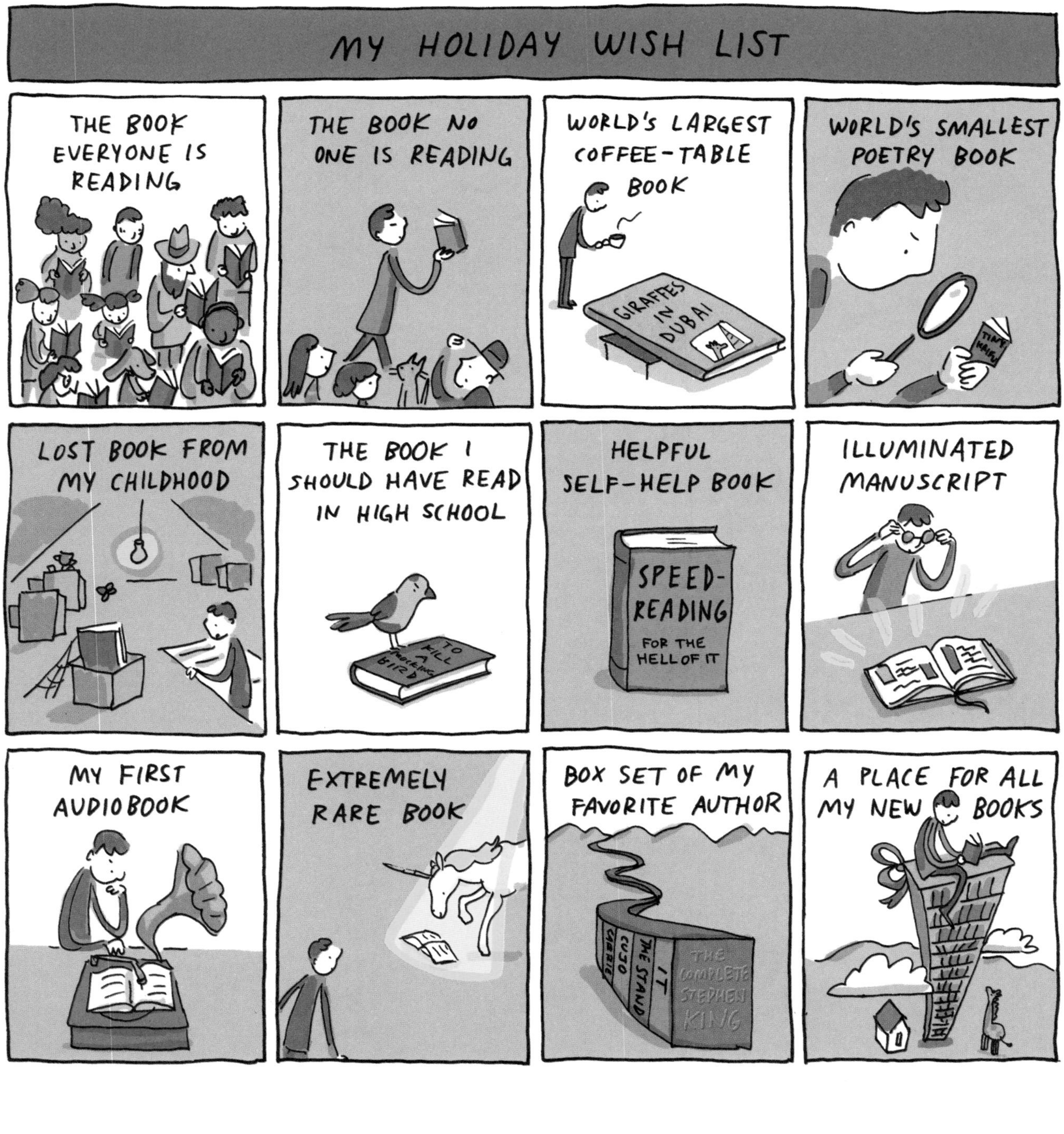

MY HOLIDAY WISH LIST
THE BOOK EVERYONE IS READING
THE BOOK NO ONE IS READING
WORLD'S LARGEST COFFEE-TABLE BOOK
GIRAFFES IN DUBAI
WORLD'S SMALLEST POETRY BOOK
TINY HAIKU
LOST BOOK FROM MY CHILDHOOD
THE BOOK I SHOULD HAVE READ IN HIGH SCHOOL
TO KILL A MOCKING BIRD
HELPFUL SELF-HELP BOOK
SPEED-READING FOR THE HELL OF IT
ILLUMINATED MANUSCRIPT
MY FIRST AUDIOBOOK
EXTREMELY RARE BOOK
BOX SET OF MY FAVORITE AUTHOR
CARRIE
CUJO
THE STAND
IT
THE COMPLETE STEPHEN KING
A PLACE FOR ALL MY NEW BOOKS

the beloved book

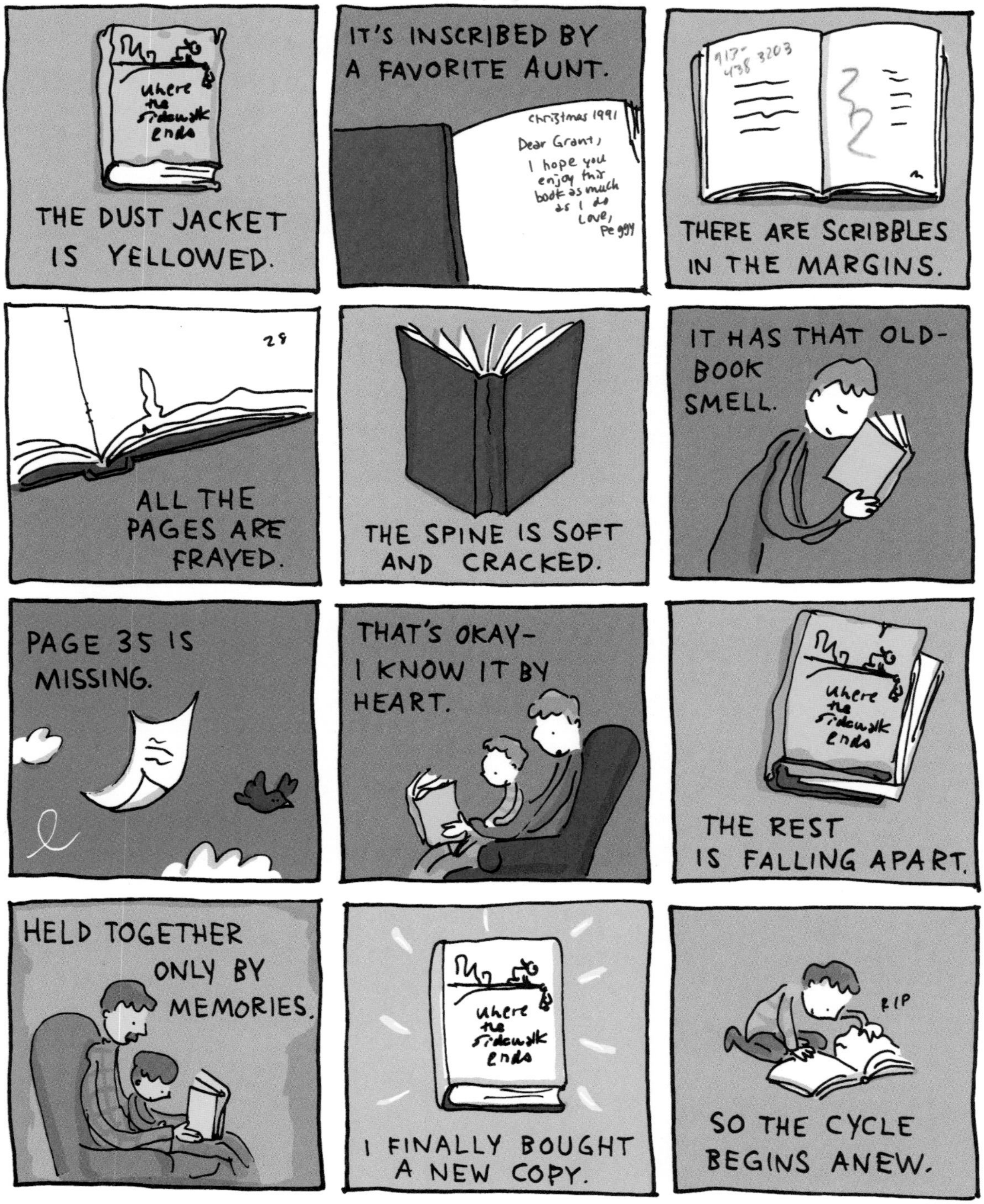

where the sidewalk ends
THE DUST JACKET IS YELLOWED.
IT'S INSCRIBED BY A FAVORITE AUNT.
Christmas 1991
Dear Grant,
I hope you enjoy this book as much as I do
Love,
Peggy
913-438 3203
THERE ARE SCRIBBLES IN THE MARGINS.
28
ALL THE PAGES ARE FRAYED.
THE SPINE IS SOFT AND CRACKED.
IT HAS THAT OLD-BOOK SMELL.
PAGE 35 IS MISSING.
THAT'S OKAY-
I KNOW IT BY HEART.
where the sidewalk ends
THE REST IS FALLING APART.
HELD TOGETHER ONLY BY MEMORIES.
where the sidewalk ends
I FINALLY BOUGHT A NEW COPY.
RIP
SO THE CYCLE BEGINS ANEW.

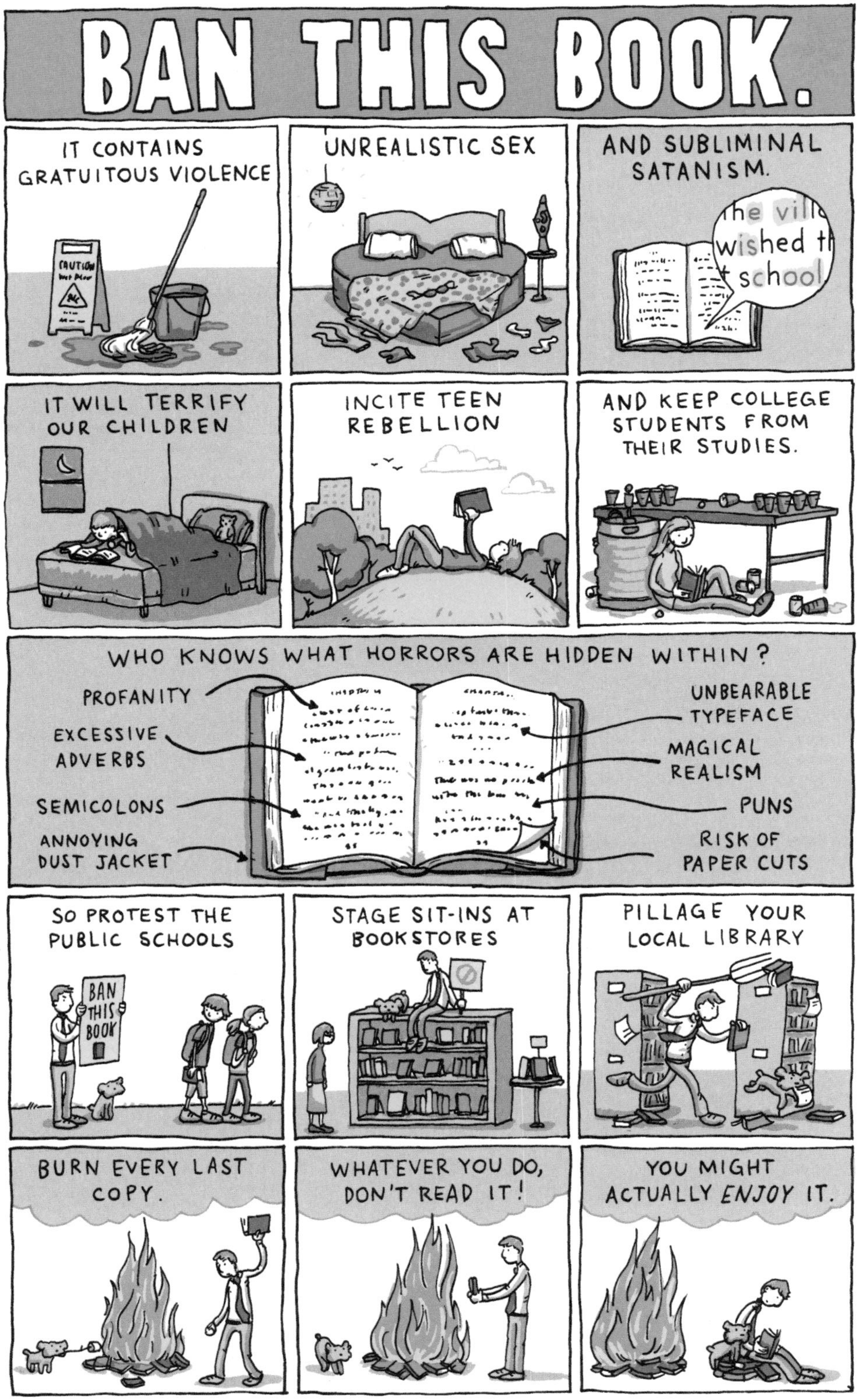
BAN THIS BOOK.
IT CONTAINS GRATUITOUS VIOLENCE
CAUTION
UNREALISTIC SEX
AND SUBLIMINAL SATANISM.
he vill
wished th
t school
IT WILL TERRIFY OUR CHILDREN
INCITE TEEN REBELLION
AND KEEP COLLEGE STUDENTS FROM THEIR STUDIES.
WHO KNOWS WHAT HORRORS ARE HIDDEN WITHIN?
PROFANITY
EXCESSIVE ADVERBS
SEMICOLONS
ANNOYING DUST JACKET
UNBEARABLE TYPEFACE
MAGICAL REALISM
PUNS
RISK OF PAPER CUTS
SO PROTEST THE PUBLIC SCHOOLS
BAN THIS BOOK
STAGE SIT-INS AT BOOKSTORES
PILLAGE YOUR LOCAL LIBRARY
BURN EVERY LAST COPY.
WHATEVER YOU DO, DON'T READ IT!
YOU MIGHT ACTUALLY *ENJOY* IT.

The Very Bad Picture Book

The weather is boring.

The colors are dull.

None of the animals can talk.

Magic doesn't work.

VOX EST TUA!

It teaches an important lesson.

SAFETY BEFORE IMAGINATION!

It tries way too hard to rhyme.

bright sun, fast run

It uses many words to say very little.

Perhaps if she waited long enough a strong wind would blow and carry her far, far away from all of her familiar surr

There is no satisfying ending.

The End.

It's almost as if... a grown-up wrote it.

41

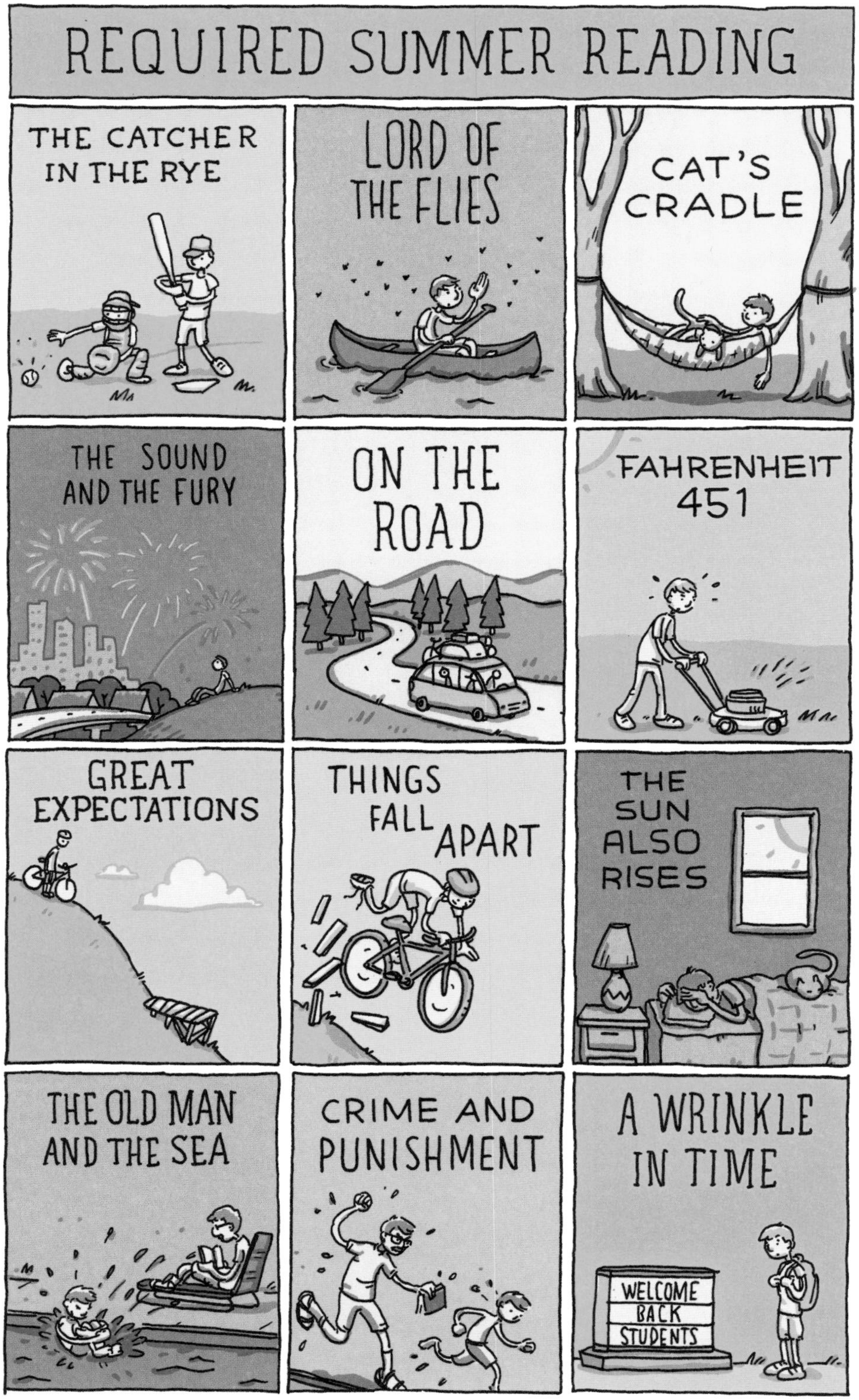
REQUIRED SUMMER READING
THE CATCHER IN THE RYE
LORD OF THE FLIES
CAT'S CRADLE
THE SOUND AND THE FURY
ON THE ROAD
FAHRENHEIT 451
GREAT EXPECTATIONS
THINGS FALL APART
THE SUN ALSO RISES
THE OLD MAN AND THE SEA
CRIME AND PUNISHMENT
A WRINKLE IN TIME
WELCOME BACK STUDENTS

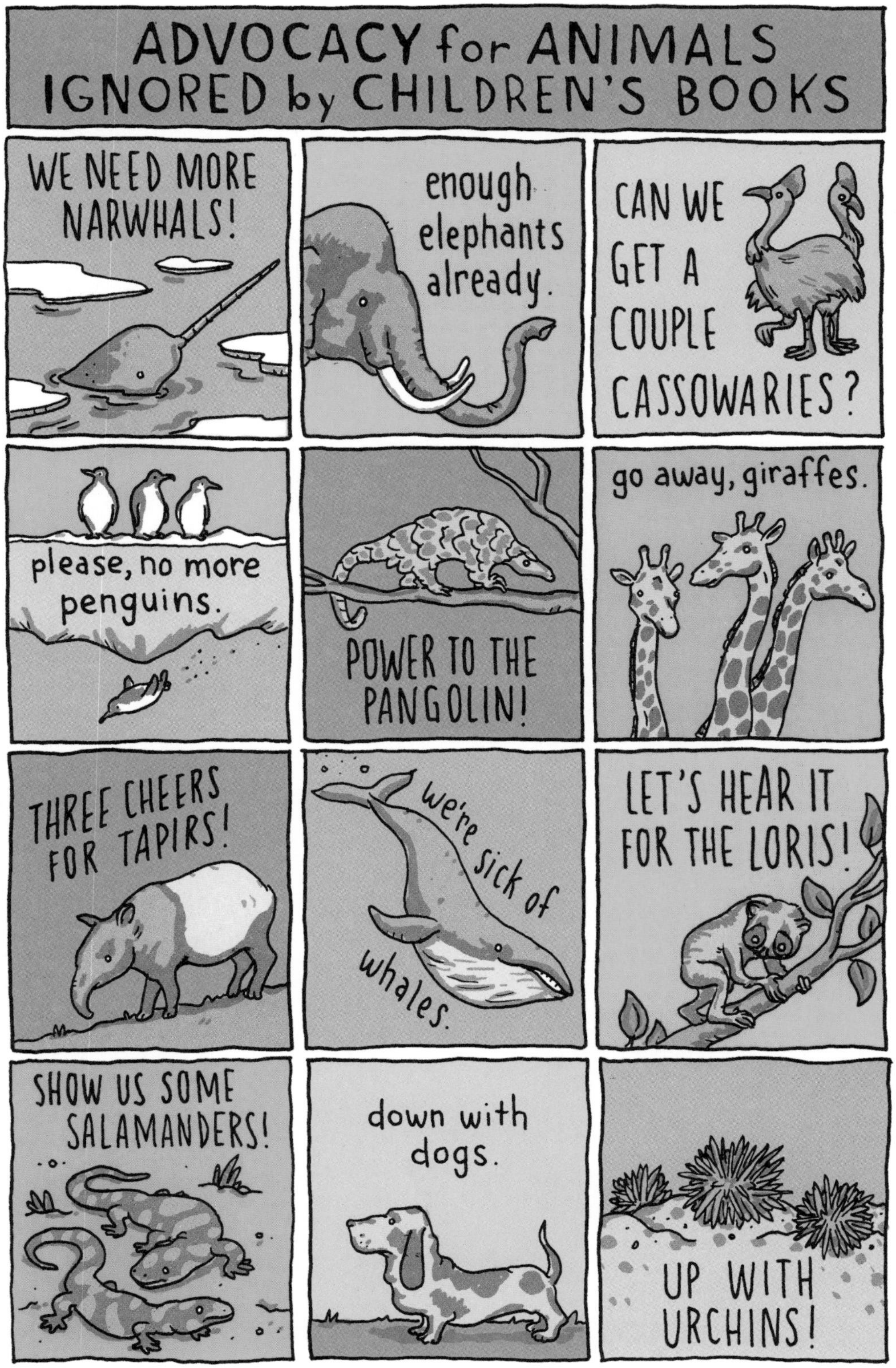
ADVOCACY for ANIMALS IGNORED by CHILDREN'S BOOKS
WE NEED MORE NARWHALS!
enough elephants already.
CAN WE GET A COUPLE CASSOWARIES?
please, no more penguins.
POWER TO THE PANGOLIN!
go away, giraffes.
THREE CHEERS FOR TAPIRS!
we're sick of whales.
LET'S HEAR IT FOR THE LORIS!
SHOW US SOME SALAMANDERS!
down with dogs.
UP WITH URCHINS!

Portrait of a Parent Reading

(AFTER GLUYAS WILLIAMS)

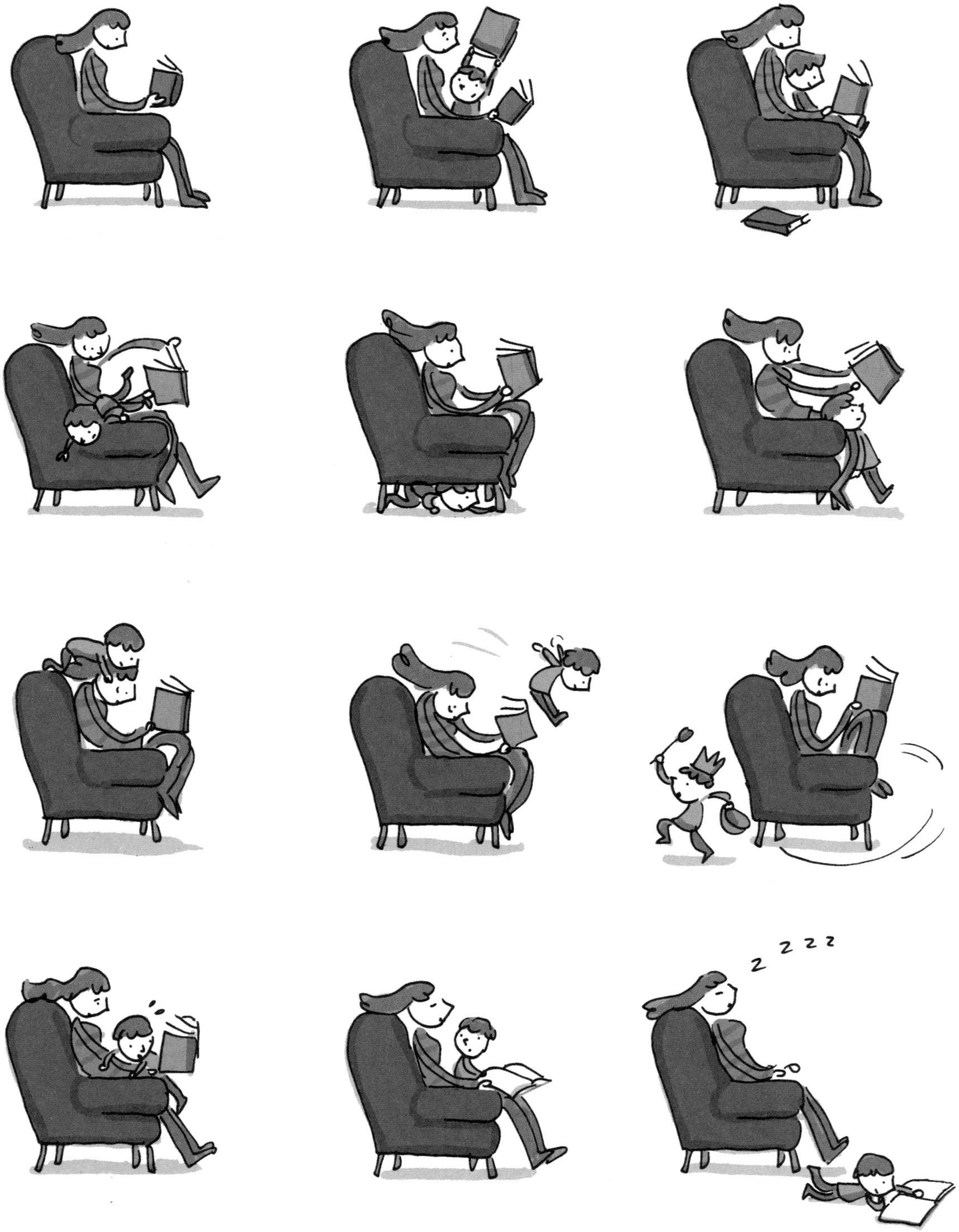
z z z z

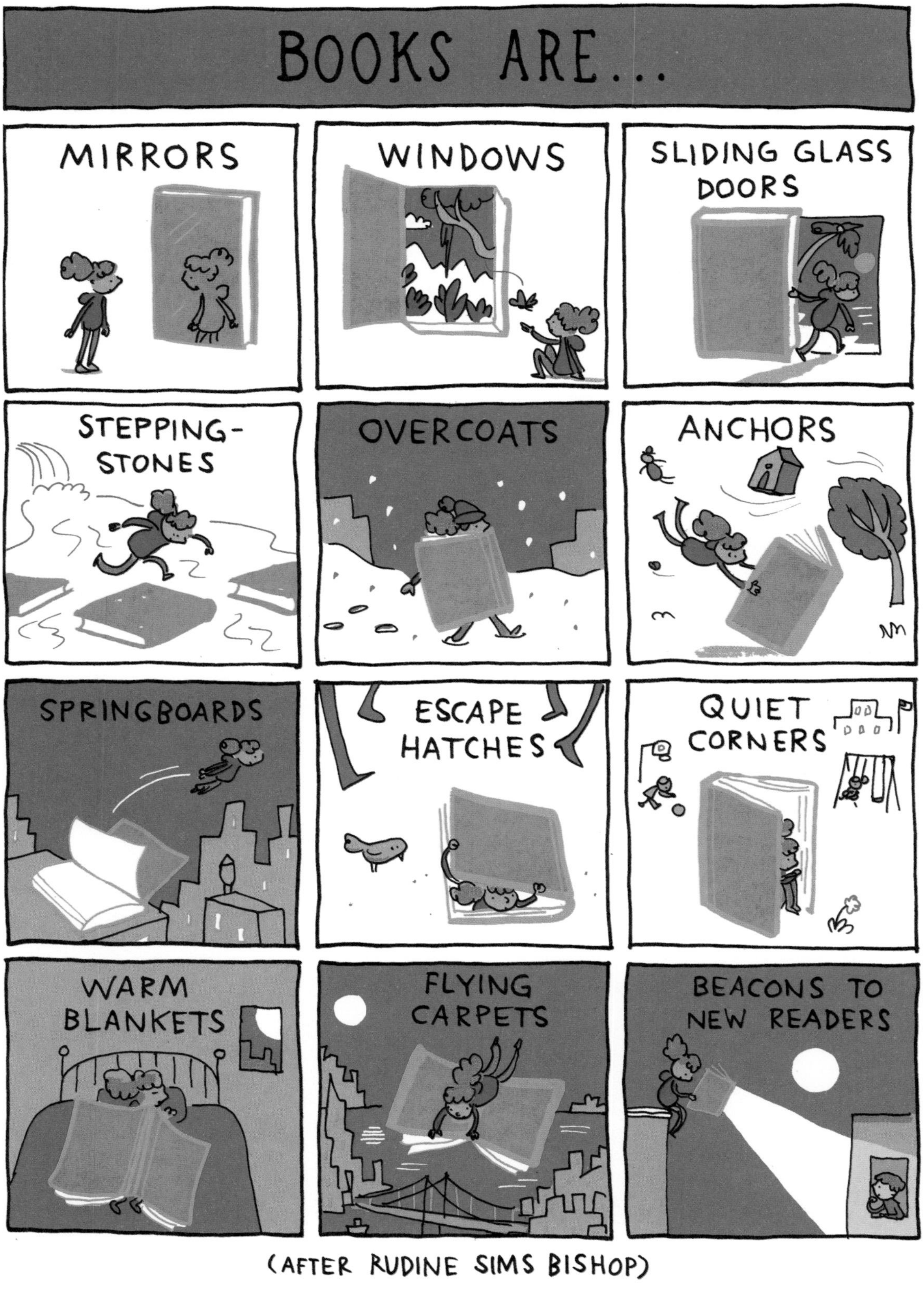
BOOKS ARE...
MIRRORS
WINDOWS
SLIDING GLASS DOORS
STEPPING-STONES
OVERCOATS
ANCHORS
SPRINGBOARDS
ESCAPE HATCHES
QUIET CORNERS
WARM BLANKETS
FLYING CARPETS
BEACONS TO NEW READERS
(AFTER RUDINE SIMS BISHOP)

THE CANNON OF LITERATURE

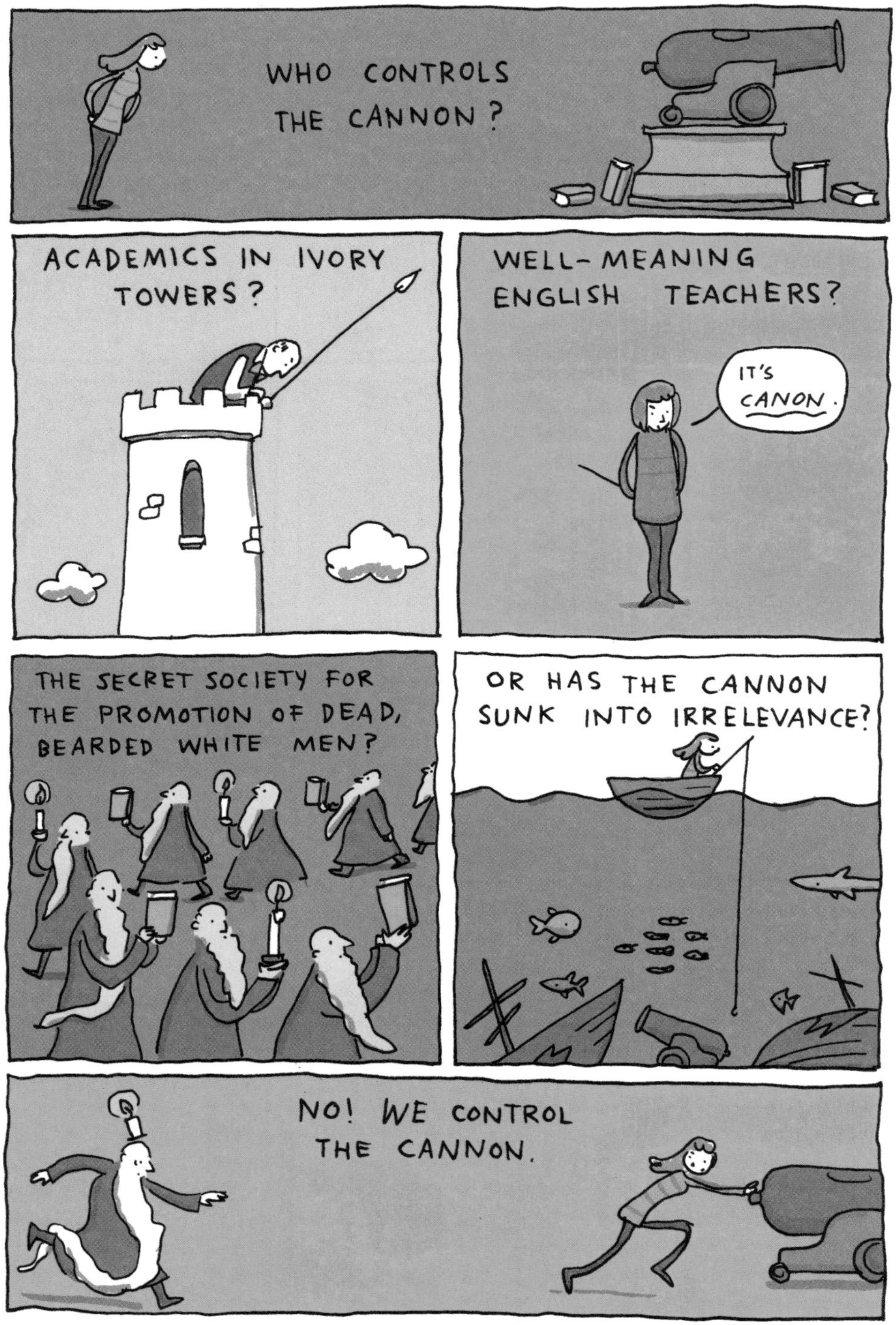
WHO CONTROLS THE CANNON?
ACADEMICS IN IVORY TOWERS?
WELL-MEANING ENGLISH TEACHERS?
IT'S CANON.
THE SECRET SOCIETY FOR THE PROMOTION OF DEAD, BEARDED WHITE MEN?
OR HAS THE CANNON SUNK INTO IRRELEVANCE?
NO! WE CONTROL THE CANNON.

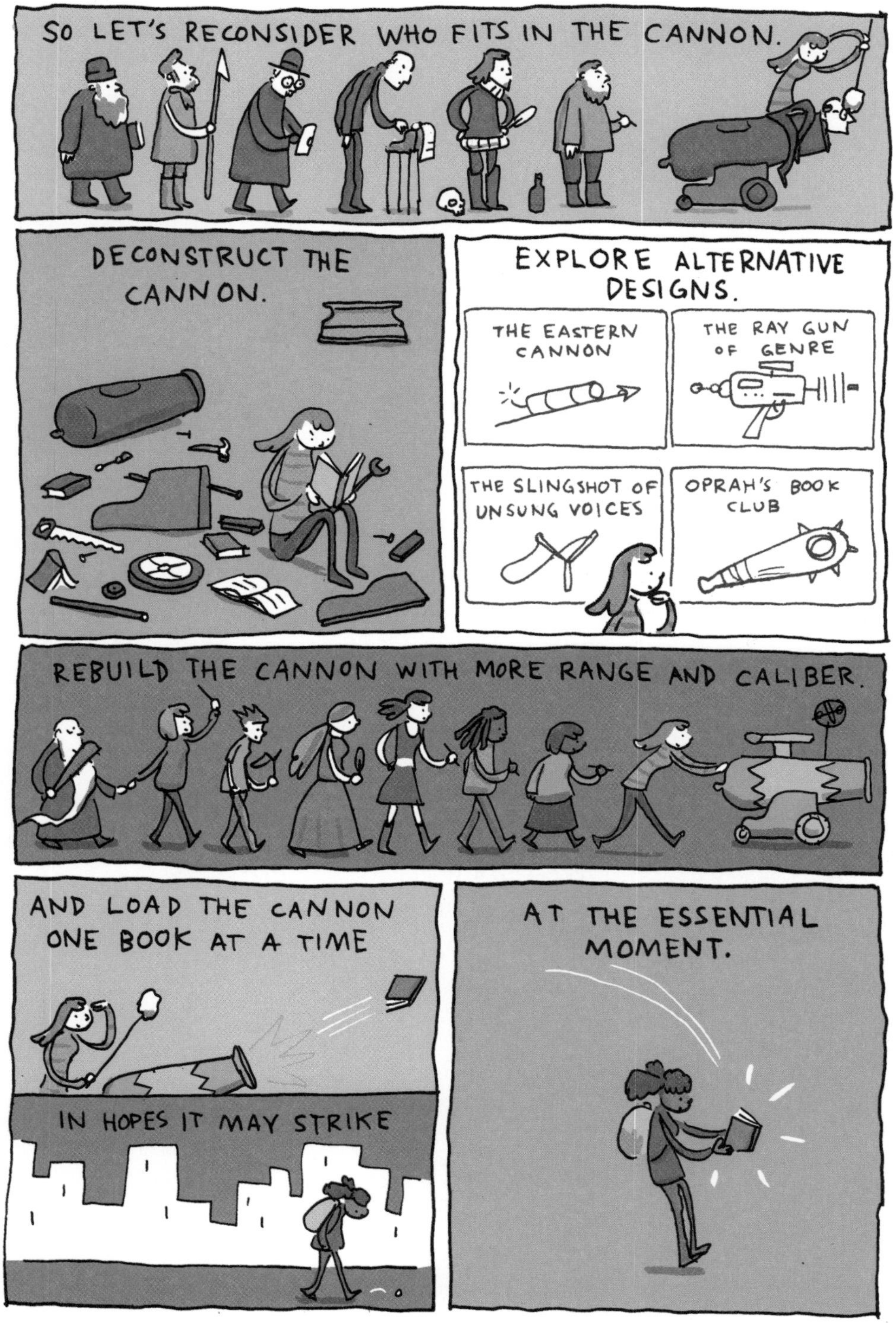
SO LET'S RECONSIDER WHO FITS IN THE CANNON.
DECONSTRUCT THE CANNON.
EXPLORE ALTERNATIVE DESIGNS.
THE EASTERN CANNON
THE RAY GUN OF GENRE
THE SLINGSHOT OF UNSUNG VOICES
OPRAH'S BOOK CLUB
REBUILD THE CANNON WITH MORE RANGE AND CALIBER.
AND LOAD THE CANNON ONE BOOK AT A TIME
IN HOPES IT MAY STRIKE
AT THE ESSENTIAL MOMENT.

I like my realism with a little bit of magic.

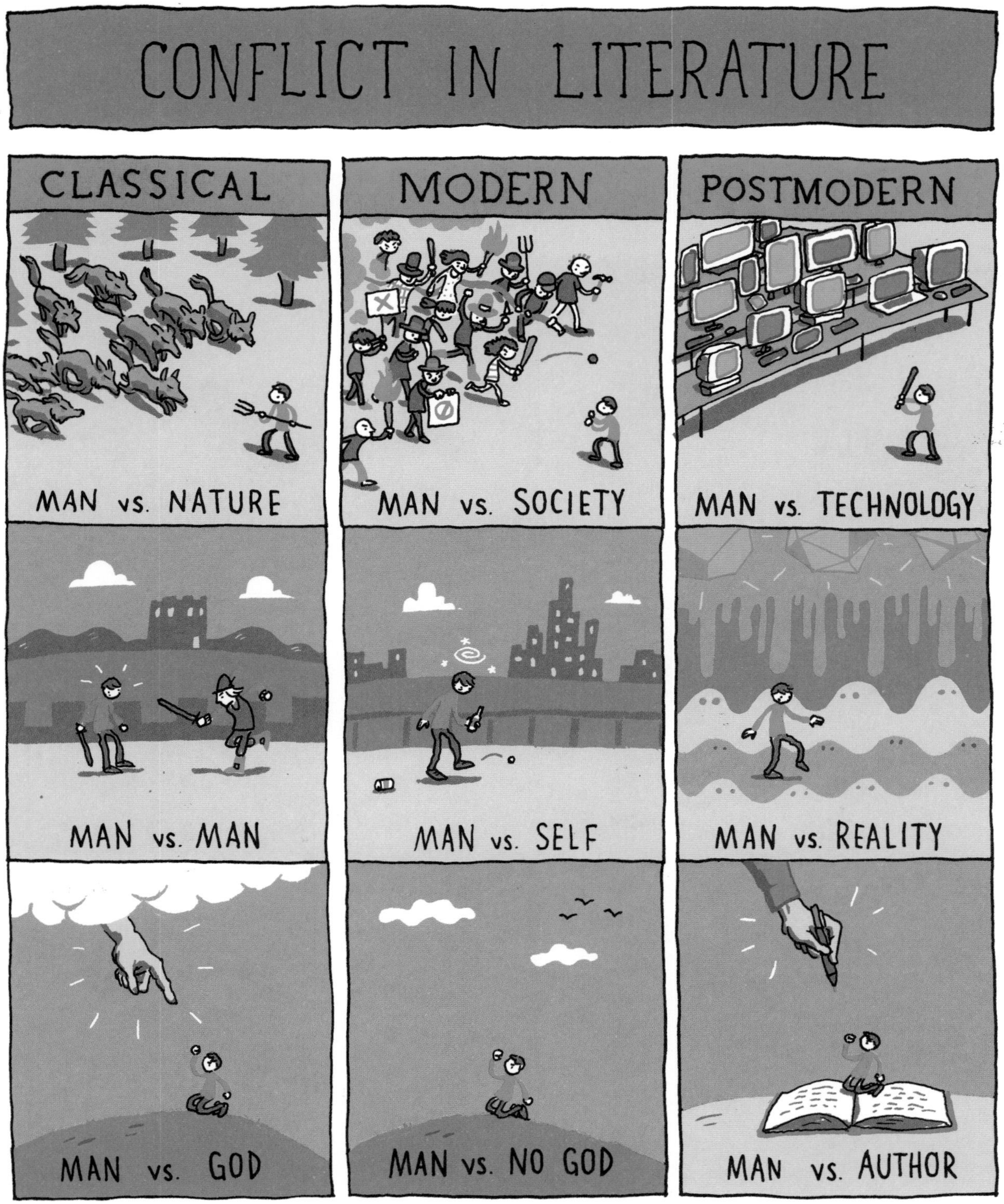
CONFLICT IN LITERATURE
CLASSICAL
MODERN
POSTMODERN
MAN vs. NATURE
MAN vs. SOCIETY
MAN vs. TECHNOLOGY
MAN vs. MAN
MAN vs. SELF
MAN vs. REALITY
MAN vs. GOD
MAN vs. NO GOD
MAN vs. AUTHOR

HARUKI MURAKAMI BINGO

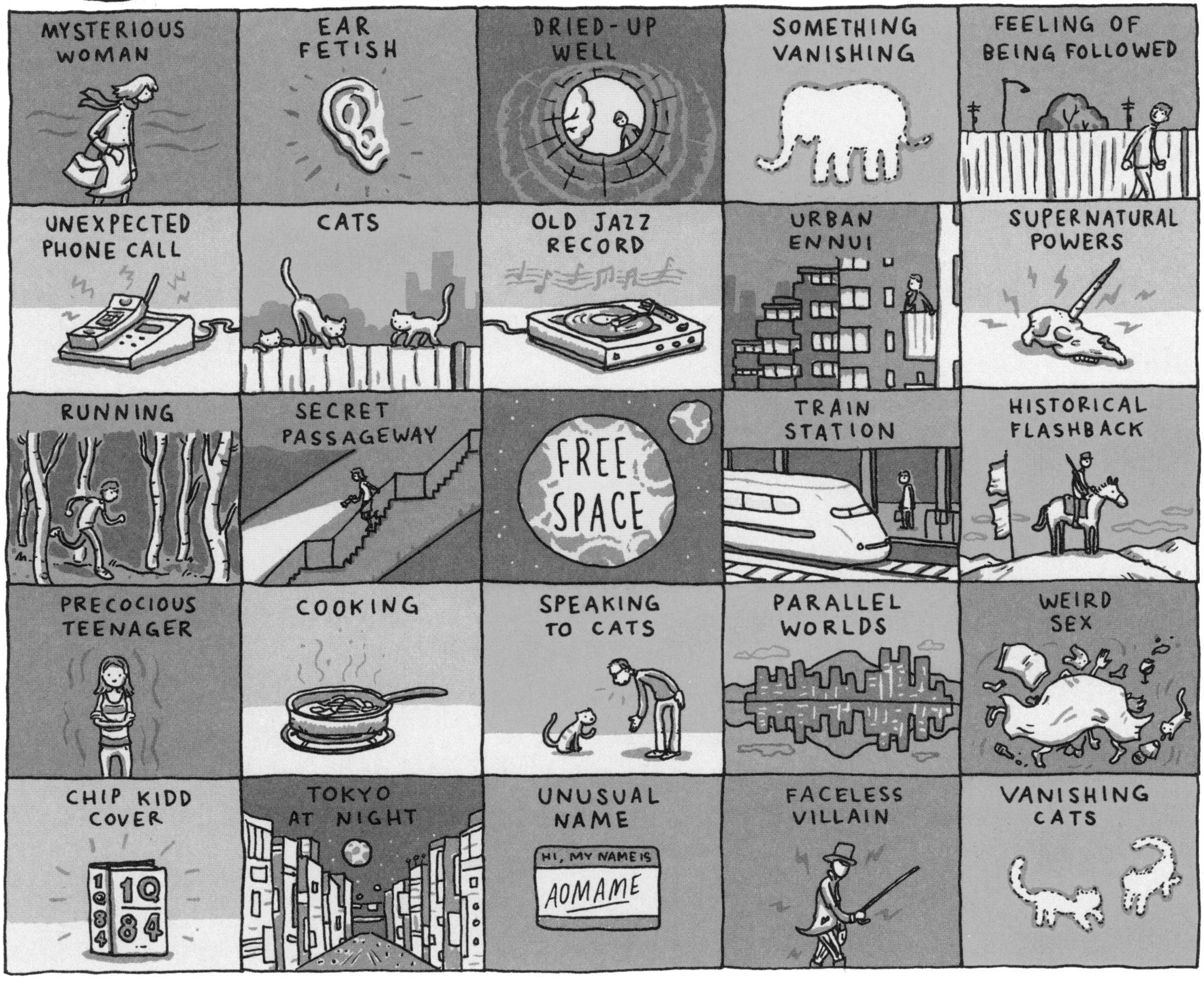

MYSTERIOUS WOMAN
EAR FETISH
DRIED-UP WELL
SOMETHING VANISHING
FEELING OF BEING FOLLOWED
UNEXPECTED PHONE CALL
CATS
OLD JAZZ RECORD
URBAN ENNUI
SUPERNATURAL POWERS
RUNNING
SECRET PASSAGEWAY
FREE SPACE
TRAIN STATION
HISTORICAL FLASHBACK
PRECOCIOUS TEENAGER
COOKING
SPEAKING TO CATS
PARALLEL WORLDS
WEIRD SEX
CHIP KIDD COVER
1Q84
TOKYO AT NIGHT
UNUSUAL NAME
HI, MY NAME IS
AOMAME
FACELESS VILLAIN
VANISHING CATS

THE ORIGINAL MANUSCRIPTS

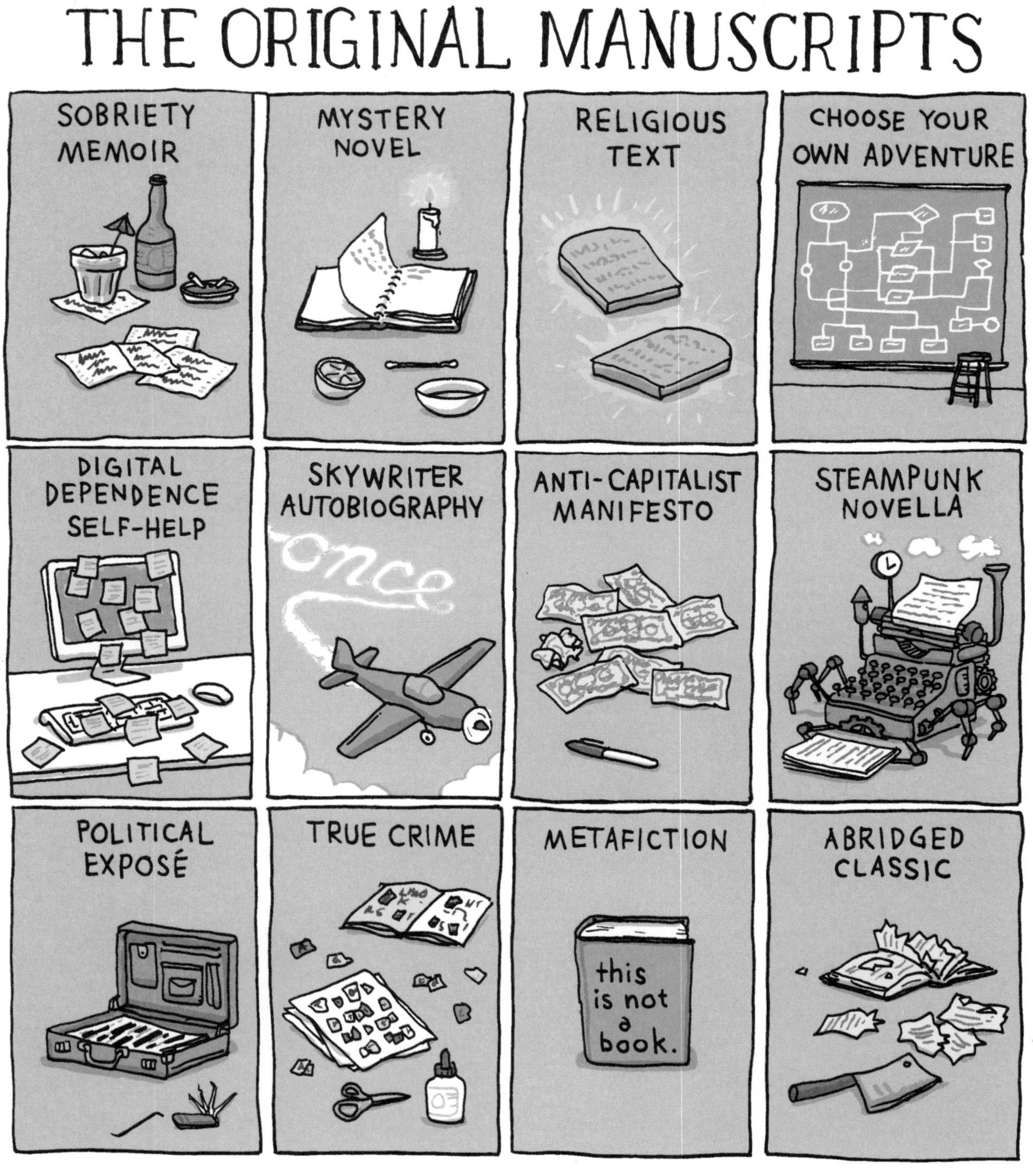
SOBRIETY MEMOIR
MYSTERY NOVEL
RELIGIOUS TEXT
CHOOSE YOUR OWN ADVENTURE
DIGITAL DEPENDENCE SELF-HELP
SKYWRITER AUTOBIOGRAPHY
once
ANTI-CAPITALIST MANIFESTO
STEAMPUNK NOVELLA
POLITICAL EXPOSÉ
TRUE CRIME
METAFICTION
this is not a book.
ABRIDGED CLASSIC

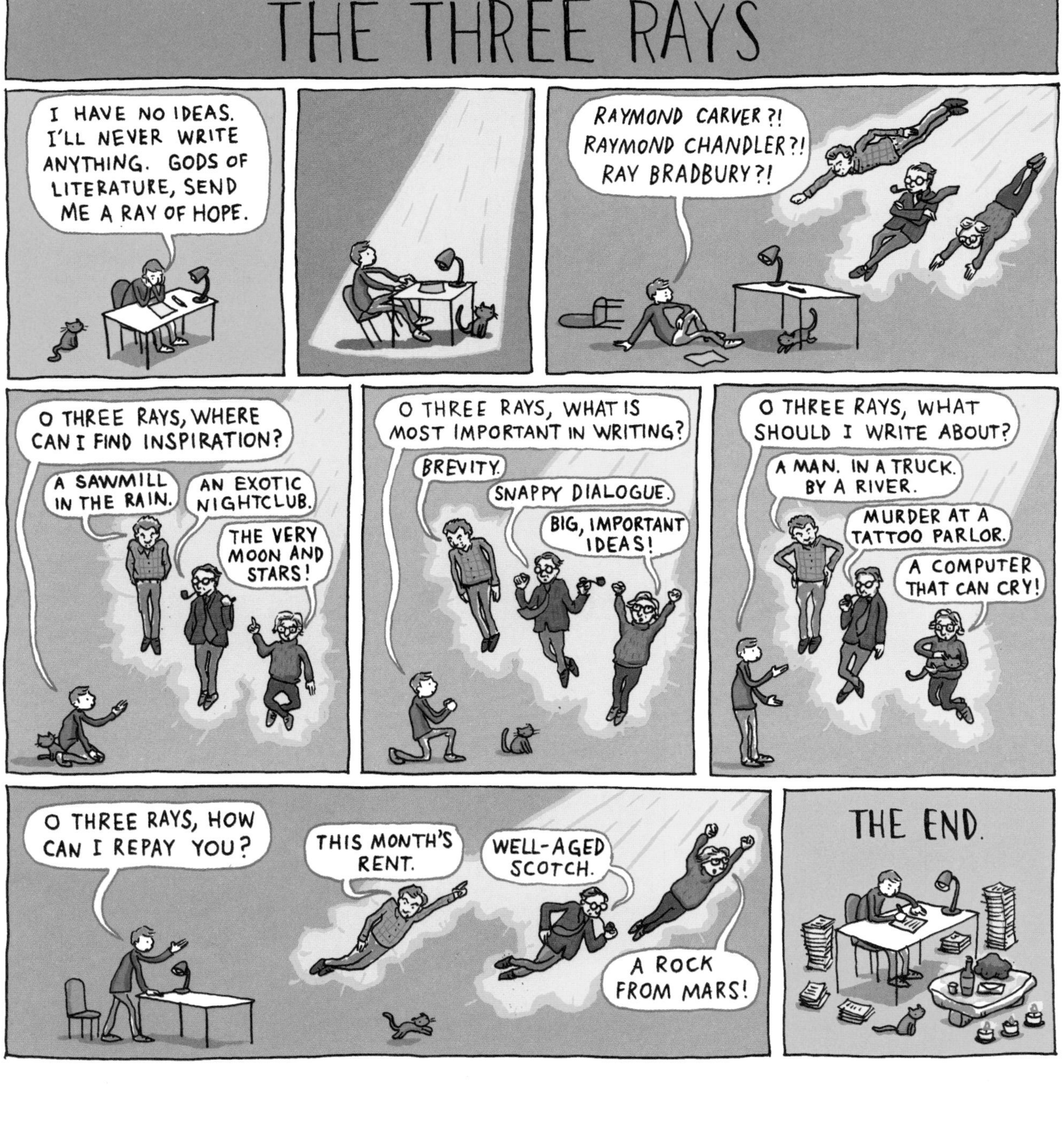
THE THREE RAYS
I HAVE NO IDEAS. I'LL NEVER WRITE ANYTHING. GODS OF LITERATURE, SEND ME A RAY OF HOPE.
RAYMOND CARVER?! RAYMOND CHANDLER?! RAY BRADBURY?!
O THREE RAYS, WHERE CAN I FIND INSPIRATION?
A SAWMILL IN THE RAIN.
AN EXOTIC NIGHTCLUB.
THE VERY MOON AND STARS!
O THREE RAYS, WHAT IS MOST IMPORTANT IN WRITING?
BREVITY.
SNAPPY DIALOGUE.
BIG, IMPORTANT IDEAS!
O THREE RAYS, WHAT SHOULD I WRITE ABOUT?
A MAN. IN A TRUCK. BY A RIVER.
MURDER AT A TATTOO PARLOR.
A COMPUTER THAT CAN CRY!
O THREE RAYS, HOW CAN I REPAY YOU?
THIS MONTH'S RENT.
WELL-AGED SCOTCH.
A ROCK FROM MARS!
THE END.

FAHRENHEIT 351

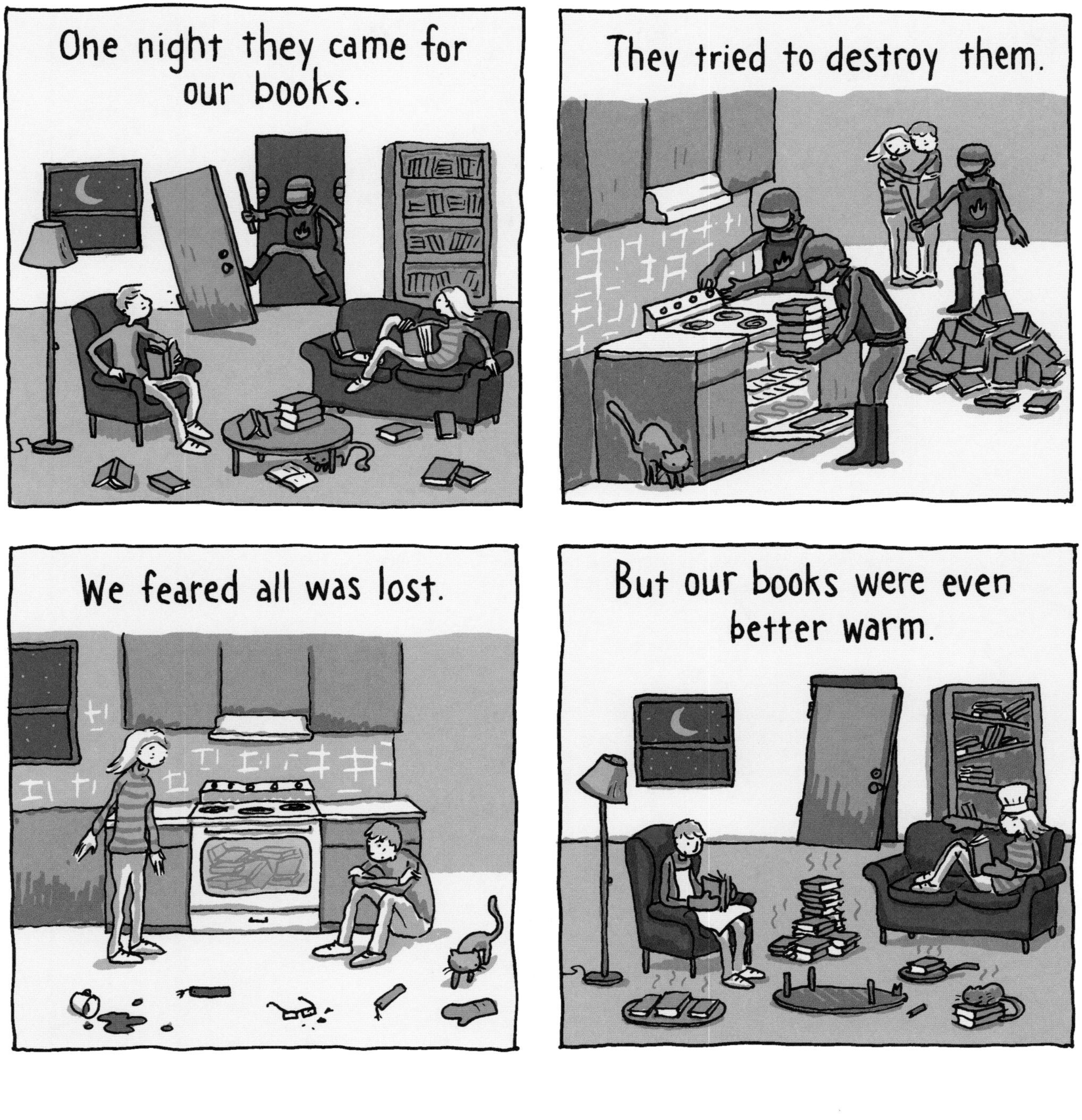
One night they came for our books.
They tried to destroy them.
We feared all was lost.
But our books were even better warm.

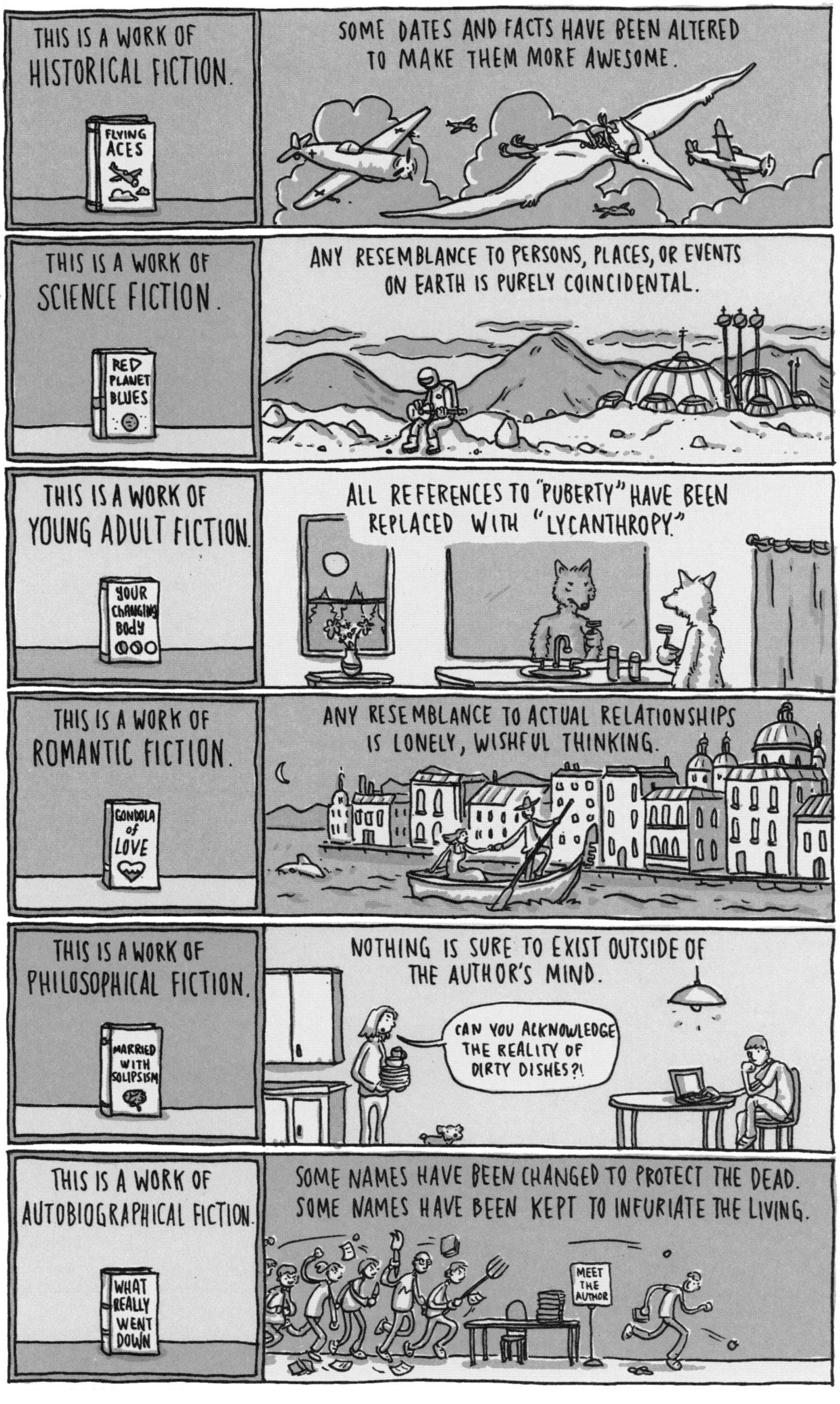
THIS IS A WORK OF HISTORICAL FICTION.
FLYING ACES
SOME DATES AND FACTS HAVE BEEN ALTERED TO MAKE THEM MORE AWESOME.
THIS IS A WORK OF SCIENCE FICTION.
RED PLANET BLUES
ANY RESEMBLANCE TO PERSONS, PLACES, OR EVENTS ON EARTH IS PURELY COINCIDENTAL.
THIS IS A WORK OF YOUNG ADULT FICTION.
YOUR CHANGING BODY
ALL REFERENCES TO "PUBERTY" HAVE BEEN REPLACED WITH "LYCANTHROPY."
THIS IS A WORK OF ROMANTIC FICTION.
GONDOLA of LOVE
ANY RESEMBLANCE TO ACTUAL RELATIONSHIPS IS LONELY, WISHFUL THINKING.
THIS IS A WORK OF PHILOSOPHICAL FICTION.
MARRIED WITH SOLIPSISM
NOTHING IS SURE TO EXIST OUTSIDE OF THE AUTHOR'S MIND.
CAN YOU ACKNOWLEDGE THE REALITY OF DIRTY DISHES?!
THIS IS A WORK OF AUTOBIOGRAPHICAL FICTION.
WHAT REALLY WENT DOWN
SOME NAMES HAVE BEEN CHANGED TO PROTECT THE DEAD. SOME NAMES HAVE BEEN KEPT TO INFURIATE THE LIVING.
MEET THE AUTHOR

STORY STRUCTURES

MURDER MYSTERY MANSION

CAUTIONARY TALE TENEMENT

FORTRESS OF FARCE

STAR-CROSSED LOVERS OBSERVATORY

COMING-OF-AGE CANTILEVER

CHOOSE YOUR OWN ADVENTURE TREE HOUSE

AQUEDUCT OF INDECIPHERABLE ALLEGORY

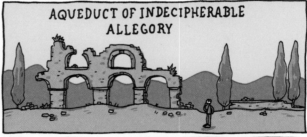

TRAGICOMEDY TENT

I like to sniff
old books.

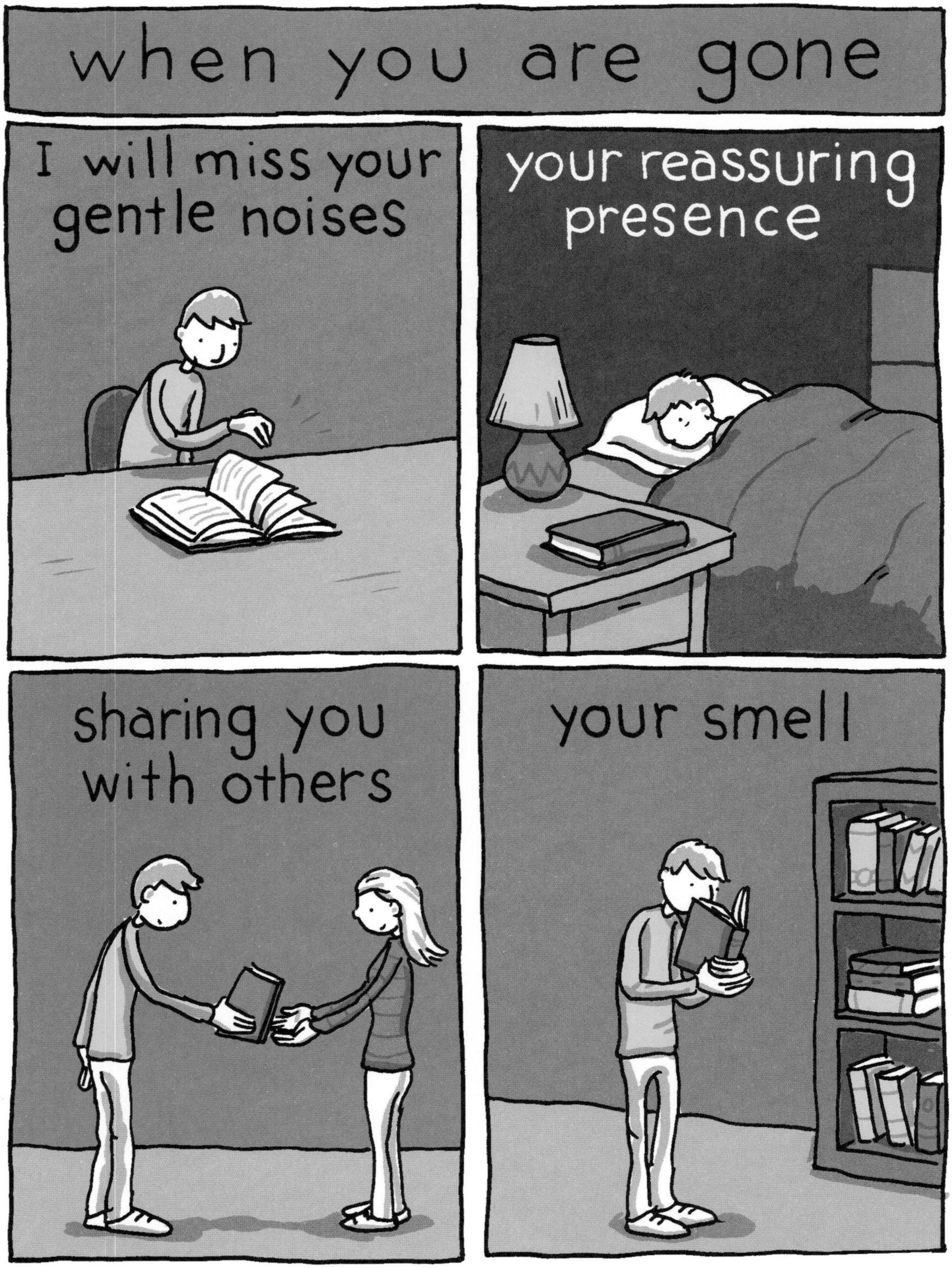
when you are gone
I will miss your gentle noises
your reassuring presence
sharing you with others
your smell

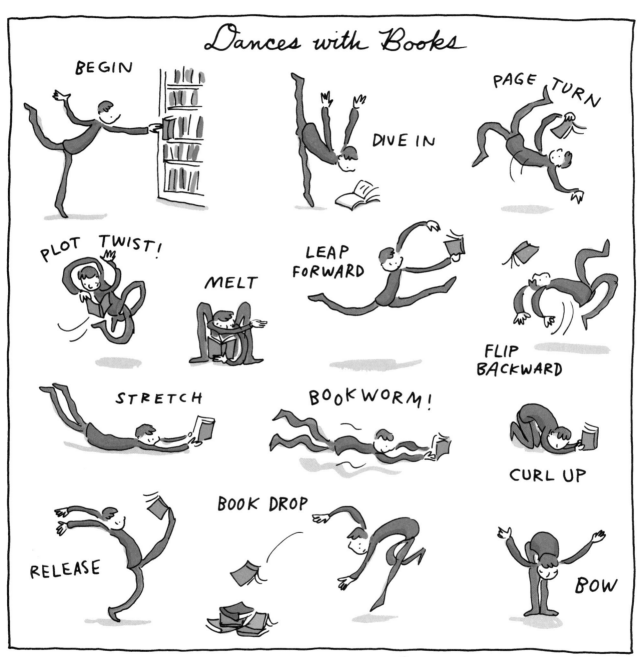

Dances with Books

BEGIN
DIVE IN
PAGE TURN
PLOT TWIST!
MELT
LEAP FORWARD
FLIP BACKWARD
STRETCH
BOOKWORM!
CURL UP
RELEASE
BOOK DROP
BOW

(AFTER REMY CHARLIP)

BOOKSHELF ORGANIZATION
FOR THE
OBSESSIVE-COMPULSIVE

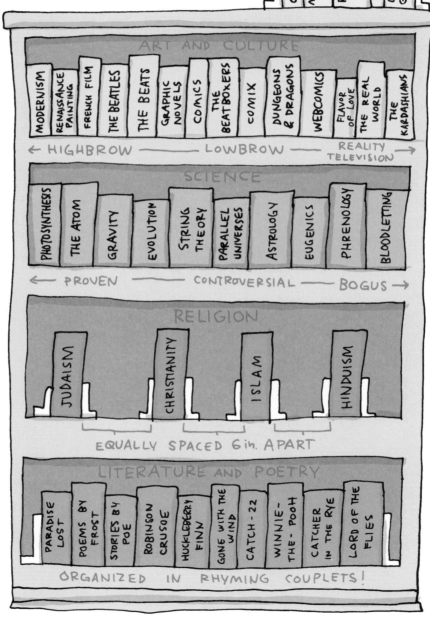

ON TALLNESS · **MANUTE BOL: A LIFE** · **RANDY NEWMAN SONGBOOK** · **GIRAFFES IN DUBAI** · **LIVING WITH GIGANTISM**

ART AND CULTURE

MODERNISM · RENAISSANCE PAINTING · FRENCH FILM · THE BEATLES · THE BEATS · GRAPHIC NOVELS · COMICS · THE BEAT BOXERS · COMIX · DUNGEONS & DRAGONS · WEBCOMICS · FLAVOR OF LOVE · THE REAL WORLD · THE KARDASHIANS

← HIGHBROW —— LOWBROW —— REALITY TELEVISION →

SCIENCE

PHOTOSYNTHESIS · THE ATOM · GRAVITY · EVOLUTION · STRING THEORY · PARALLEL UNIVERSES · ASTROLOGY · EUGENICS · PHRENOLOGY · BLOODLETTING

← PROVEN —— CONTROVERSIAL —— BOGUS →

RELIGION

JUDAISM · CHRISTIANITY · ISLAM · HINDUISM

EQUALLY SPACED 6 in. APART

LITERATURE AND POETRY

PARADISE LOST · POEMS BY FROST · STORIES BY POE · ROBINSON CRUSOE · HUCKLEBERRY FINN · GONE WITH THE WIND · CATCH-22 · WINNIE-THE-POOH · CATCHER IN THE RYE · LORD OF THE FLIES

ORGANIZED IN RHYMING COUPLETS!

THE BOOK OF THE FUTURE

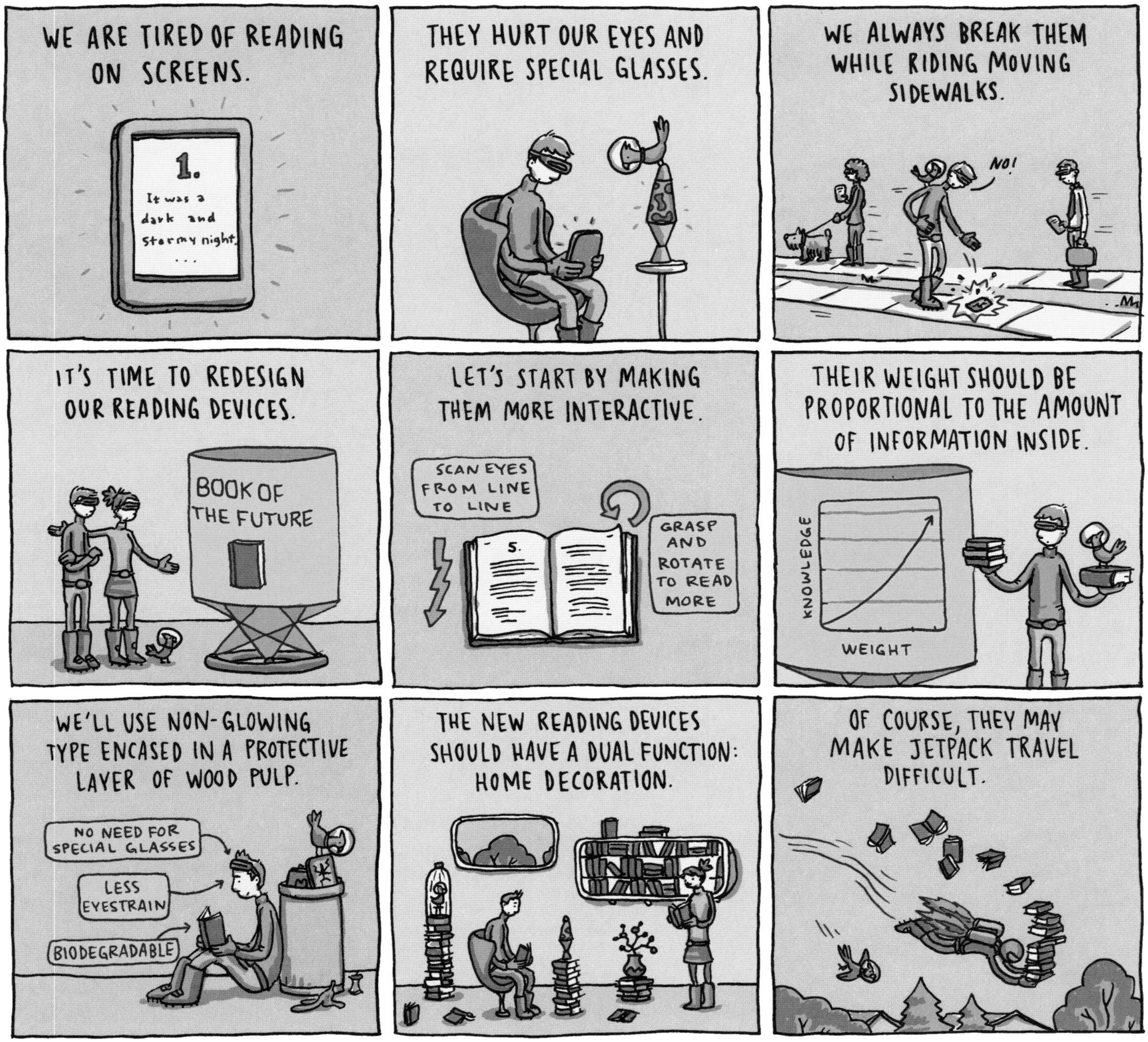
WE ARE TIRED OF READING ON SCREENS.
1.
It was a dark and stormy night, ...
THEY HURT OUR EYES AND REQUIRE SPECIAL GLASSES.
WE ALWAYS BREAK THEM WHILE RIDING MOVING SIDEWALKS.
NO!
IT'S TIME TO REDESIGN OUR READING DEVICES.
BOOK OF THE FUTURE
LET'S START BY MAKING THEM MORE INTERACTIVE.
SCAN EYES FROM LINE TO LINE
5.
GRASP AND ROTATE TO READ MORE
THEIR WEIGHT SHOULD BE PROPORTIONAL TO THE AMOUNT OF INFORMATION INSIDE.
KNOWLEDGE
WEIGHT
WE'LL USE NON-GLOWING TYPE ENCASED IN A PROTECTIVE LAYER OF WOOD PULP.
NO NEED FOR SPECIAL GLASSES
LESS EYESTRAIN
BIODEGRADABLE
THE NEW READING DEVICES SHOULD HAVE A DUAL FUNCTION: HOME DECORATION.
OF COURSE, THEY MAY MAKE JETPACK TRAVEL DIFFICULT.

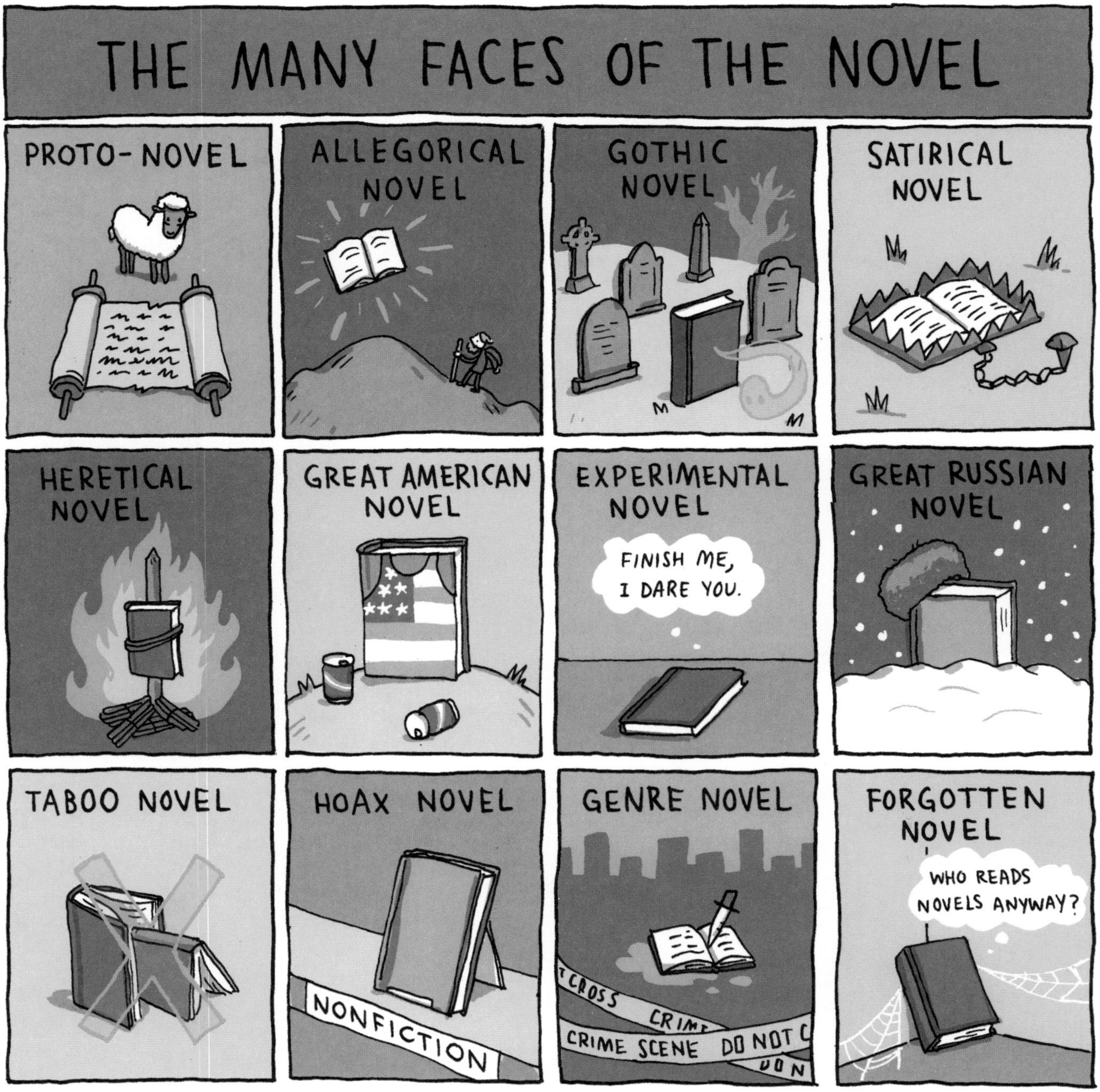
THE MANY FACES OF THE NOVEL
PROTO-NOVEL
ALLEGORICAL NOVEL
GOTHIC NOVEL
SATIRICAL NOVEL
HERETICAL NOVEL
GREAT AMERICAN NOVEL
EXPERIMENTAL NOVEL
FINISH ME, I DARE YOU.
GREAT RUSSIAN NOVEL
TABOO NOVEL
HOAX NOVEL
NONFICTION
GENRE NOVEL
CROSS
CRIME SCENE DO NOT C
FORGOTTEN NOVEL
WHO READS NOVELS ANYWAY?

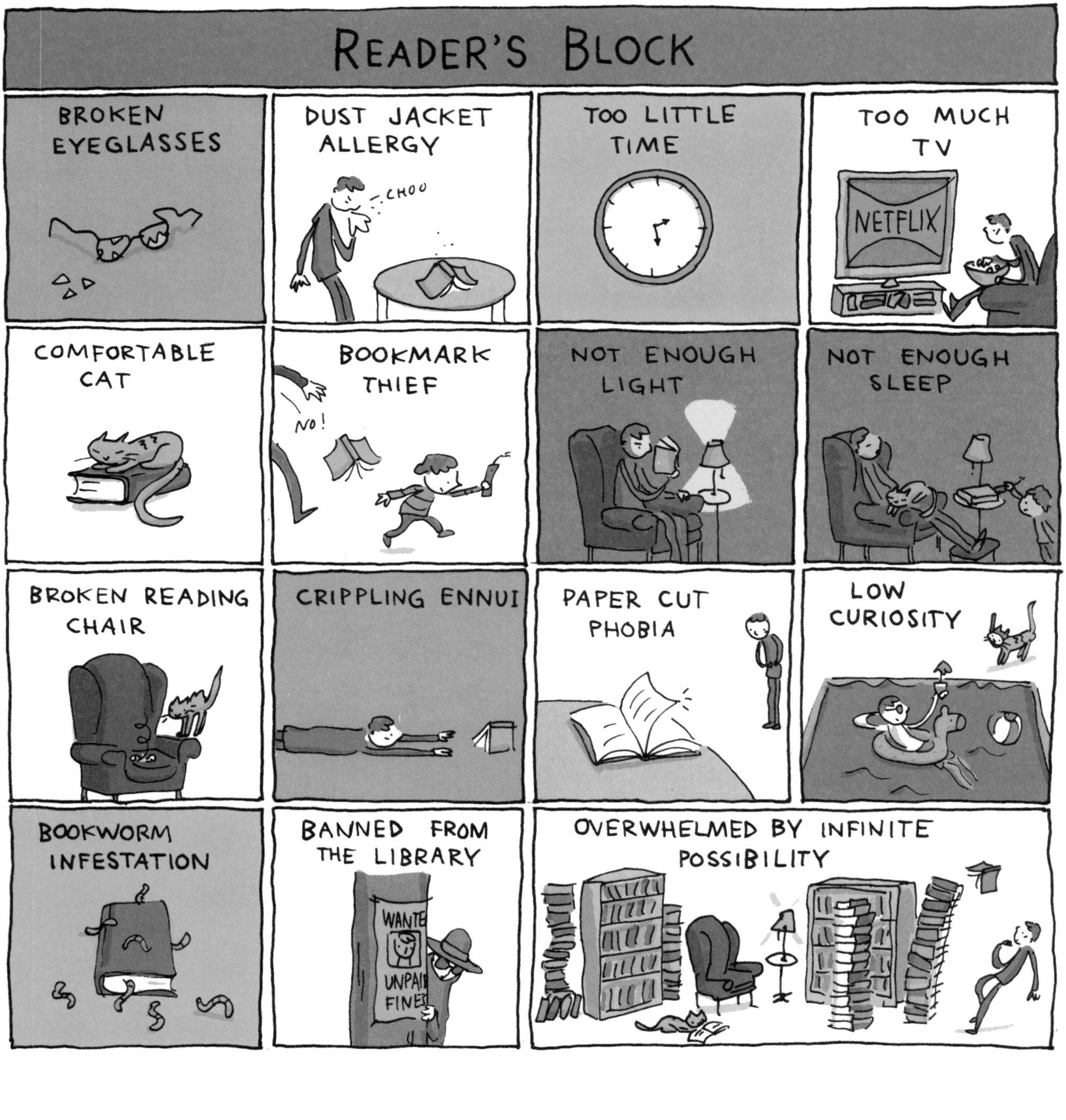
READER'S BLOCK
BROKEN EYEGLASSES
DUST JACKET ALLERGY
-CHOO
TOO LITTLE TIME
TOO MUCH TV
NETFLIX
COMFORTABLE CAT
BOOKMARK THIEF
NO!
NOT ENOUGH LIGHT
NOT ENOUGH SLEEP
BROKEN READING CHAIR
CRIPPLING ENNUI
PAPER CUT PHOBIA
LOW CURIOSITY
BOOKWORM INFESTATION
BANNED FROM THE LIBRARY
WANTE
UNPAI
FINES
OVERWHELMED BY INFINITE POSSIBILITY

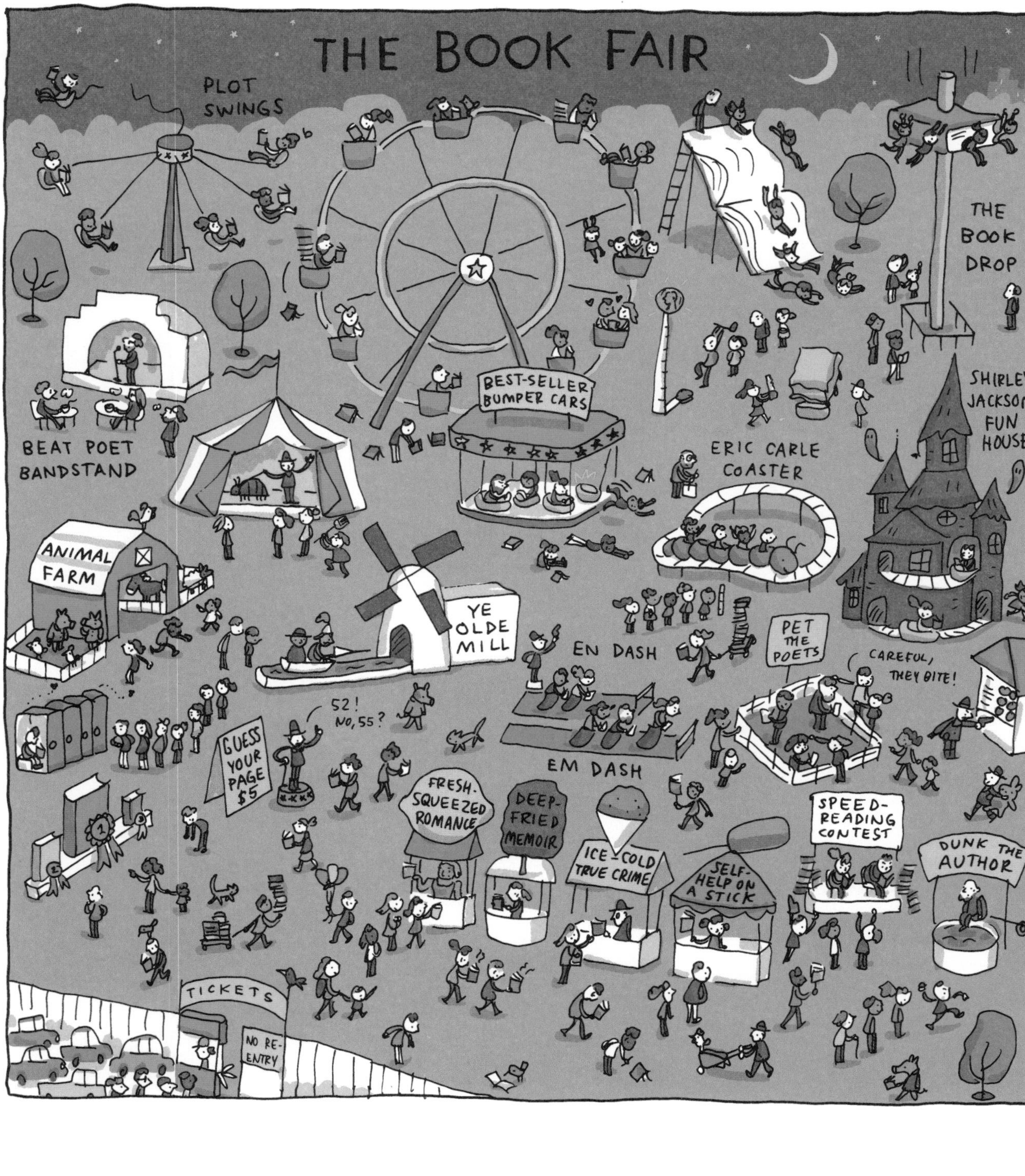
THE BOOK FAIR
PLOT SWINGS
THE BOOK DROP
BEAT POET BANDSTAND
BEST-SELLER BUMPER CARS
SHIRLEY JACKSON FUN HOUSE
ERIC CARLE COASTER
ANIMAL FARM
YE OLDE MILL
EN DASH
PET THE POETS
CAREFUL, THEY BITE!
52! NO, 55?
GUESS YOUR PAGE $5
EM DASH
FRESH-SQUEEZED ROMANCE
DEEP-FRIED MEMOIR
ICE-COLD TRUE CRIME
SELF-HELP ON A STICK
SPEED-READING CONTEST
DUNK THE AUTHOR
TICKETS
NO RE-ENTRY

I am
searching for
a miracle cure
for writer's
block.

advice to writers

PUT PAPER (BLANK) TO PENCIL (SHARP).

TRY TO MAKE SPARKS.

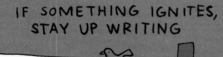

IF SOMETHING IGNITES, STAY UP WRITING

BY THE FIRE YOUR WORDS ARE LIGHTING.

IF BY MORNING, YOU END UP CHARRED—

DON'T GIVE UP. WRITING'S HARD.

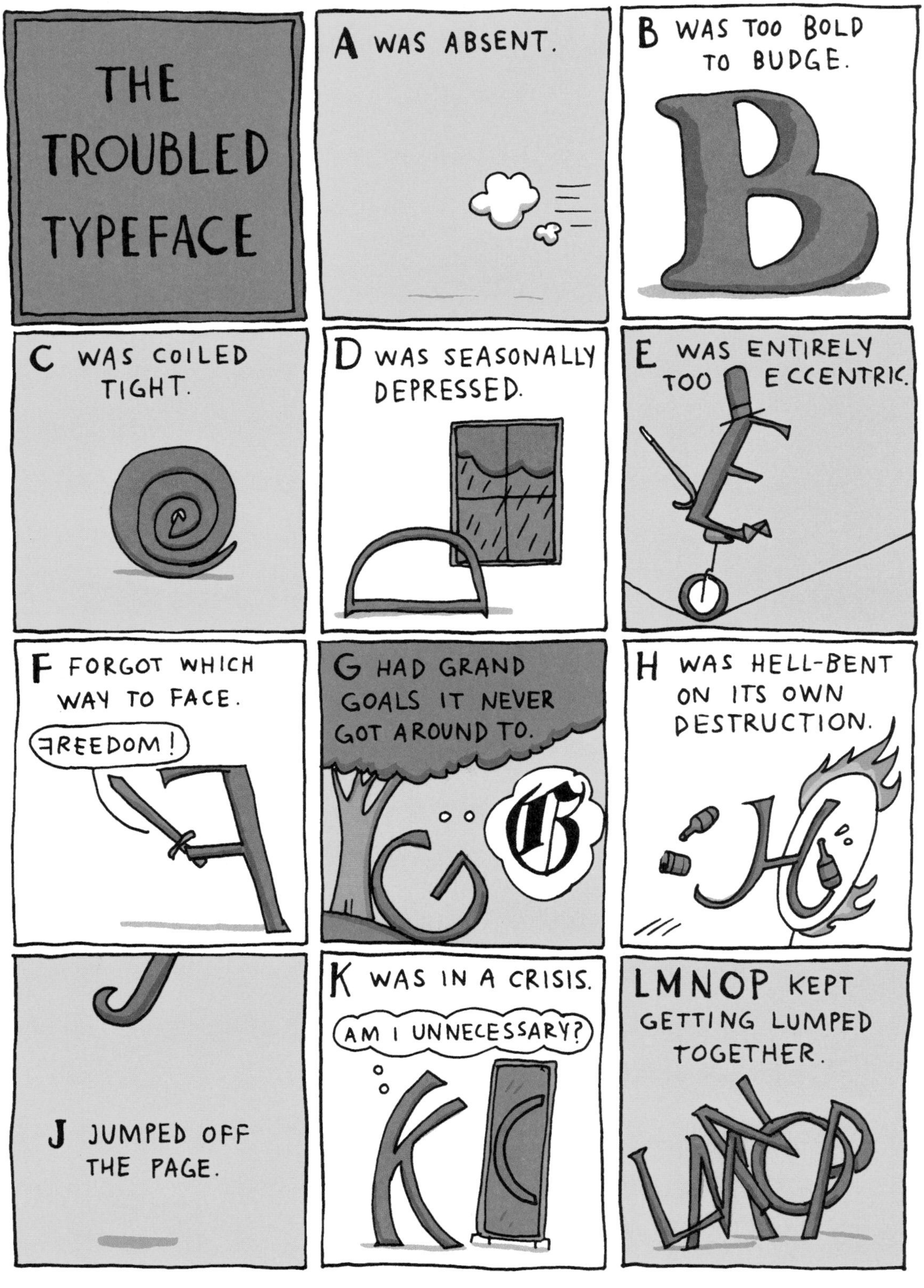
THE TROUBLED TYPEFACE
A WAS ABSENT.
B WAS TOO BOLD TO BUDGE.
C WAS COILED TIGHT.
D WAS SEASONALLY DEPRESSED.
E WAS ENTIRELY TOO ECCENTRIC.
F FORGOT WHICH WAY TO FACE.
ƎREEDOM!
G HAD GRAND GOALS IT NEVER GOT AROUND TO.
H WAS HELL-BENT ON ITS OWN DESTRUCTION.
J JUMPED OFF THE PAGE.
K WAS IN A CRISIS.
AM I UNNECESSARY?
LMNOP KEPT GETTING LUMPED TOGETHER.

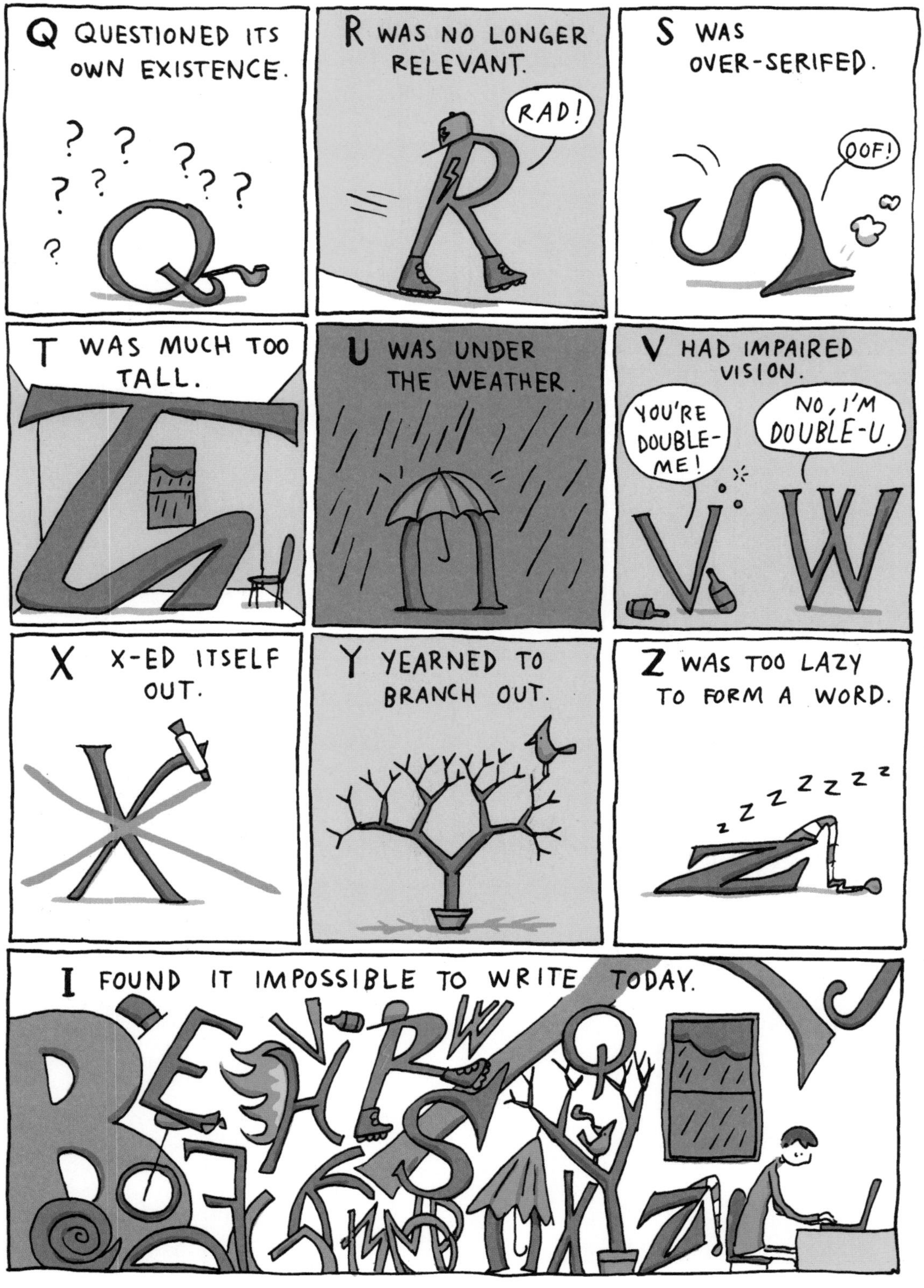
Q QUESTIONED ITS OWN EXISTENCE.
R WAS NO LONGER RELEVANT.
RAD!
S WAS OVER-SERIFED.
OOF!
T WAS MUCH TOO TALL.
U WAS UNDER THE WEATHER.
V HAD IMPAIRED VISION.
YOU'RE DOUBLE-ME!
NO, I'M DOUBLE-U.
X X-ED ITSELF OUT.
Y YEARNED TO BRANCH OUT.
Z WAS TOO LAZY TO FORM A WORD.
I FOUND IT IMPOSSIBLE TO WRITE TODAY.

Mindfulness

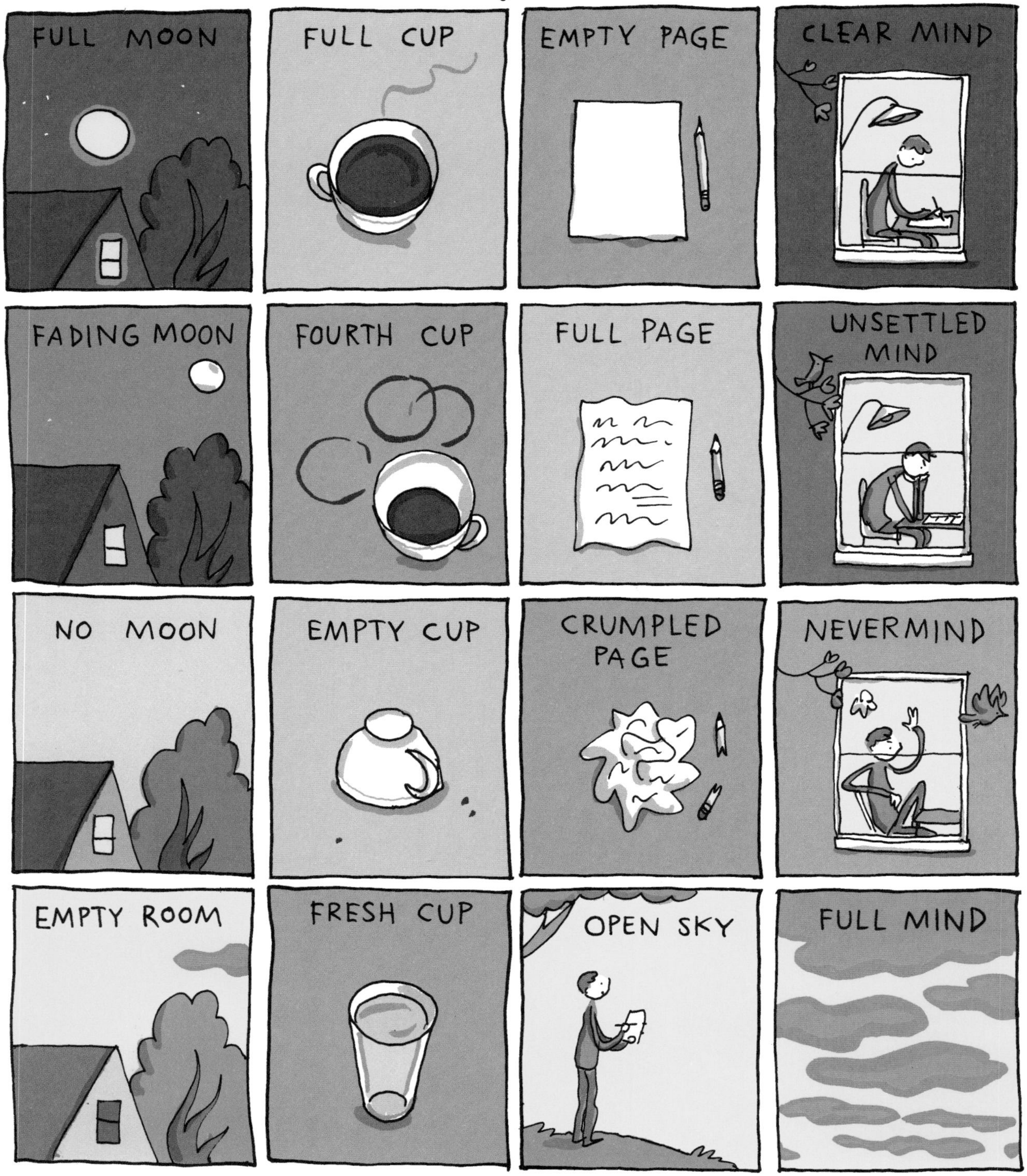
FULL MOON
FULL CUP
EMPTY PAGE
CLEAR MIND
FADING MOON
FOURTH CUP
FULL PAGE
UNSETTLED MIND
NO MOON
EMPTY CUP
CRUMPLED PAGE
NEVERMIND
EMPTY ROOM
FRESH CUP
OPEN SKY
FULL MIND

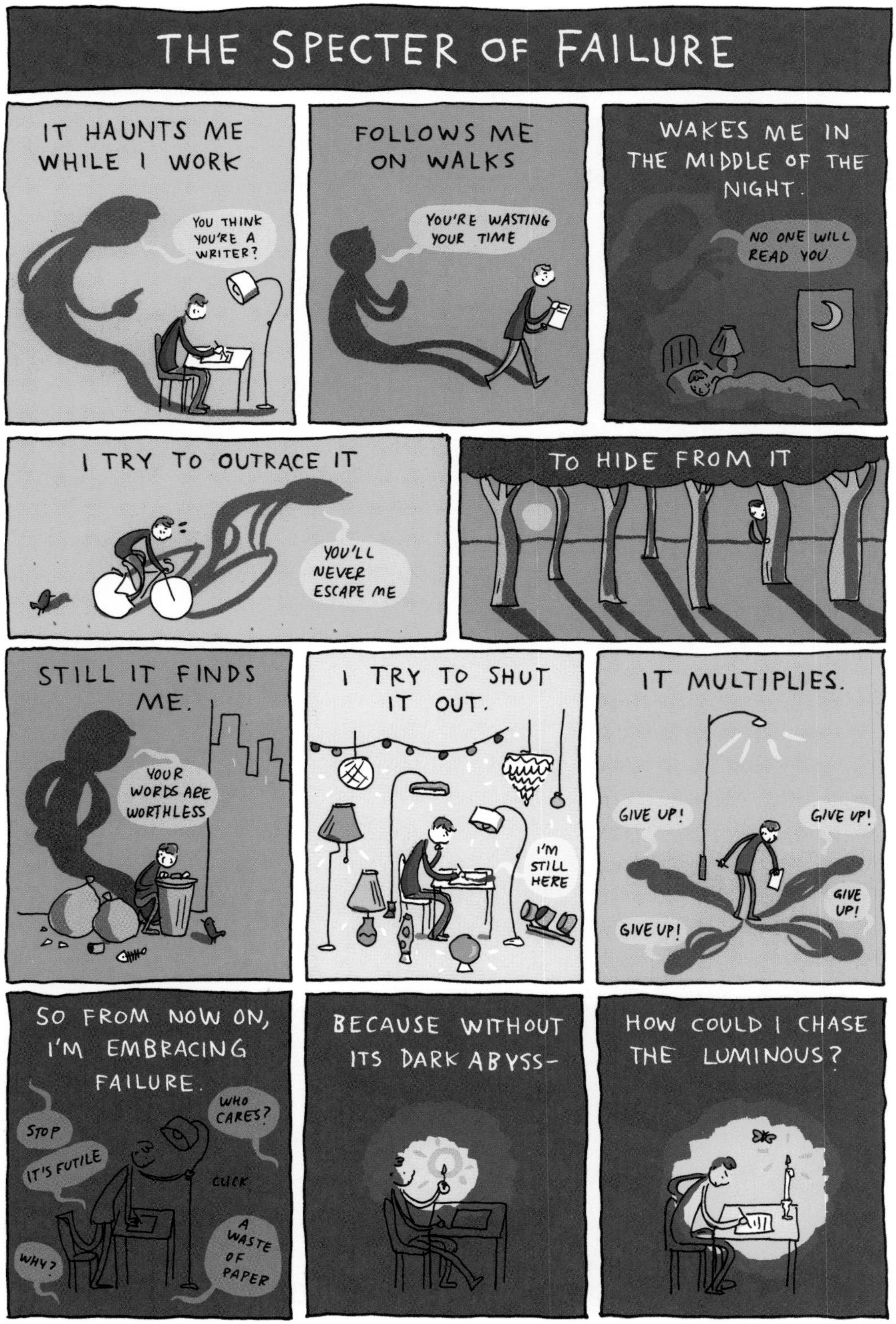
THE SPECTER OF FAILURE
IT HAUNTS ME WHILE I WORK
YOU THINK YOU'RE A WRITER?
FOLLOWS ME ON WALKS
YOU'RE WASTING YOUR TIME
WAKES ME IN THE MIDDLE OF THE NIGHT.
NO ONE WILL READ YOU
I TRY TO OUTRACE IT
YOU'LL NEVER ESCAPE ME
TO HIDE FROM IT
STILL IT FINDS ME.
YOUR WORDS ARE WORTHLESS
I TRY TO SHUT IT OUT.
I'M STILL HERE
IT MULTIPLIES.
GIVE UP!
GIVE UP!
GIVE UP!
GIVE UP!
SO FROM NOW ON, I'M EMBRACING FAILURE.
STOP
WHO CARES?
IT'S FUTILE
CLICK
WHY?
A WASTE OF PAPER
BECAUSE WITHOUT ITS DARK ABYSS-
HOW COULD I CHASE THE LUMINOUS?

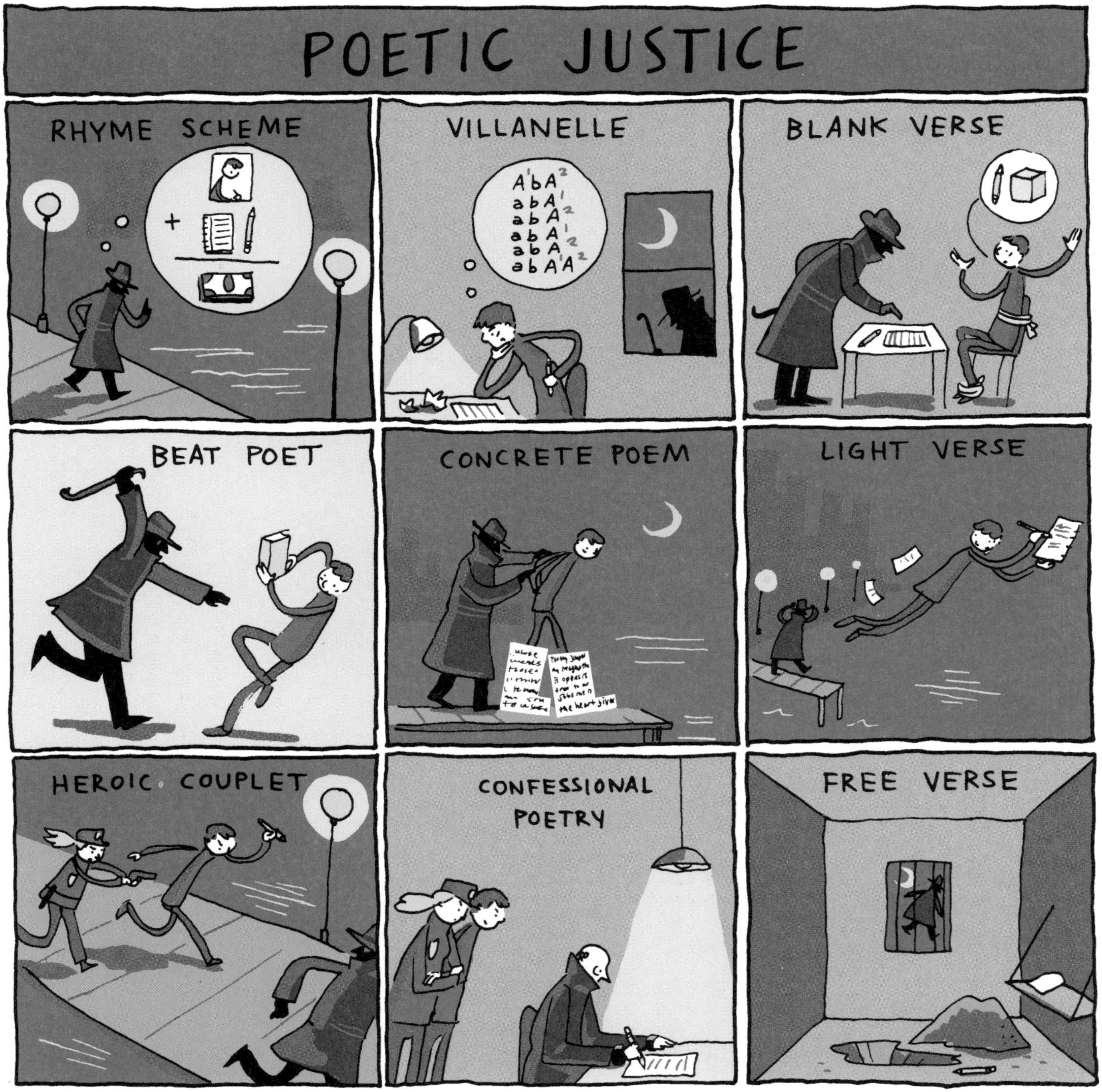
POETIC JUSTICE
RHYME SCHEME
VILLANELLE
BLANK VERSE
BEAT POET
CONCRETE POEM
LIGHT VERSE
HEROIC COUPLET
CONFESSIONAL POETRY
FREE VERSE

Literary Consolation Prizes

THICK BOOK AWARD 	**MEDAL OF GRAMMAR** 	**FIRST NOVEL ENCOURAGEMENT STICKERS** 	**UNPUBLISHED AUTHOR PIZZA PARTY** 
FORMERLY PRECOCIOUS WRITER ISSUE 	**UNNECESSARY PUNCTUATION RIBBON** 	**SELF-PROCLAIMED GENIUS GRANT** 	**LOVECRAFT PRIZE FOR ZOMBIE FICTION** 
EPIC TRILOGY COMPLETION TALISMAN 	**OVERINFLATED AMBITION BALLOON** 	**CERTIFICATE OF AUTHENTICITY** 	**PARTICIPATION TROPHY** 

I care about
punctuation—
a lot.

Proofreader's Marks

e	Delete	∧	Add mustache
(ital)	Set in italics	[stet]	And a Stetson hat
(ital)	Set in Italy	∼	Curl mustache
(rom)	Preferably in Rome	⌣	Flying mustache!
⊙⊙⊙	Insert ellipsis	‵‵ ‶	More drama
⊙	Insert cyclopsis	◎◎	More hypnosis
(wf)	Wrong font	#	Insert space
(wtf)	Horribly wrong font	=	Write faster
. . . . Ant problem		Got bored, played tic-tac-toe
Insert colon		Word tornado
"Good grief!"		

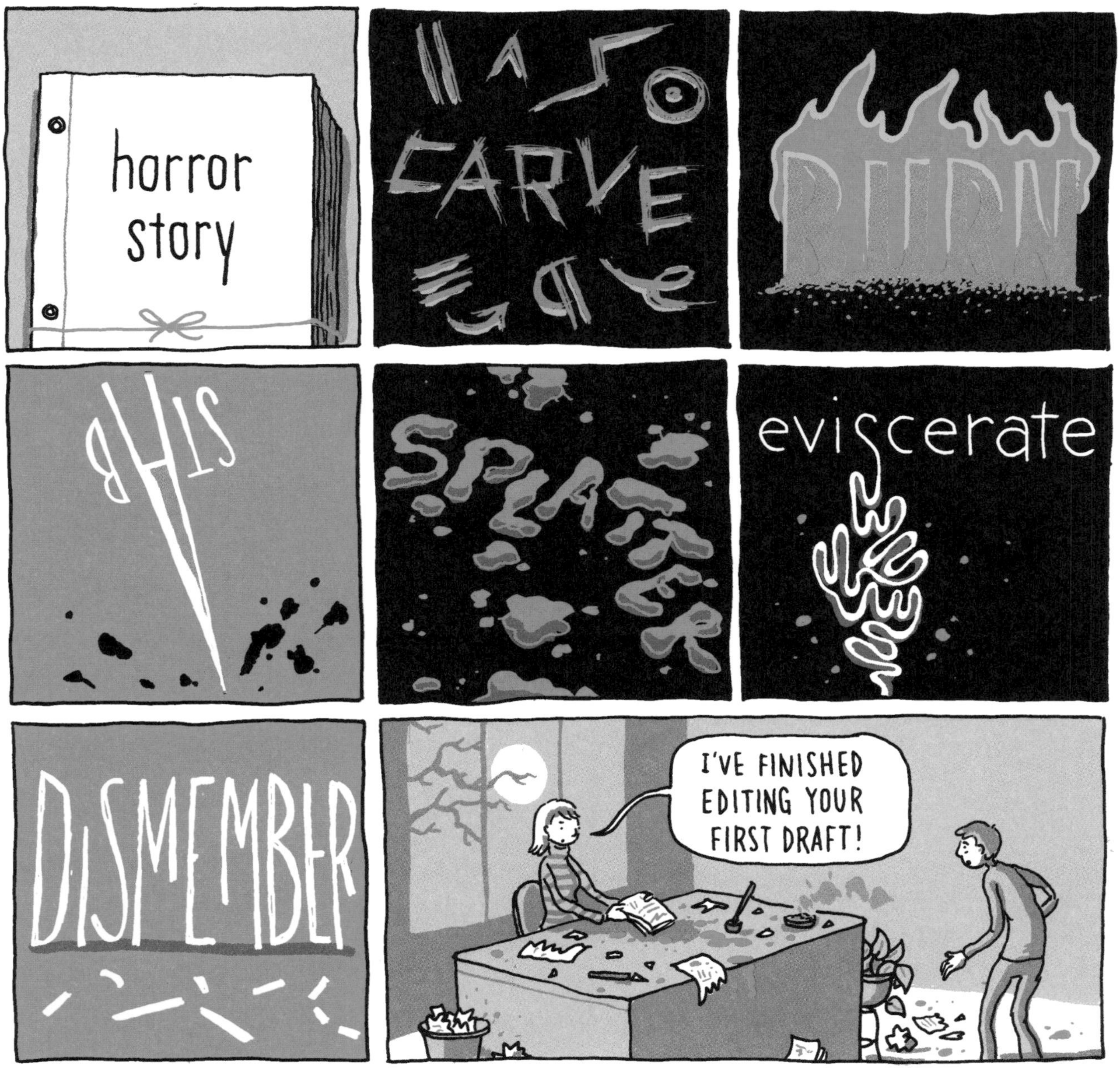
horror story
CARVE
BURN
STAB
SPLATTER
eviscerate
DISMEMBER
I'VE FINISHED EDITING YOUR FIRST DRAFT!

SUMMER NIGHT

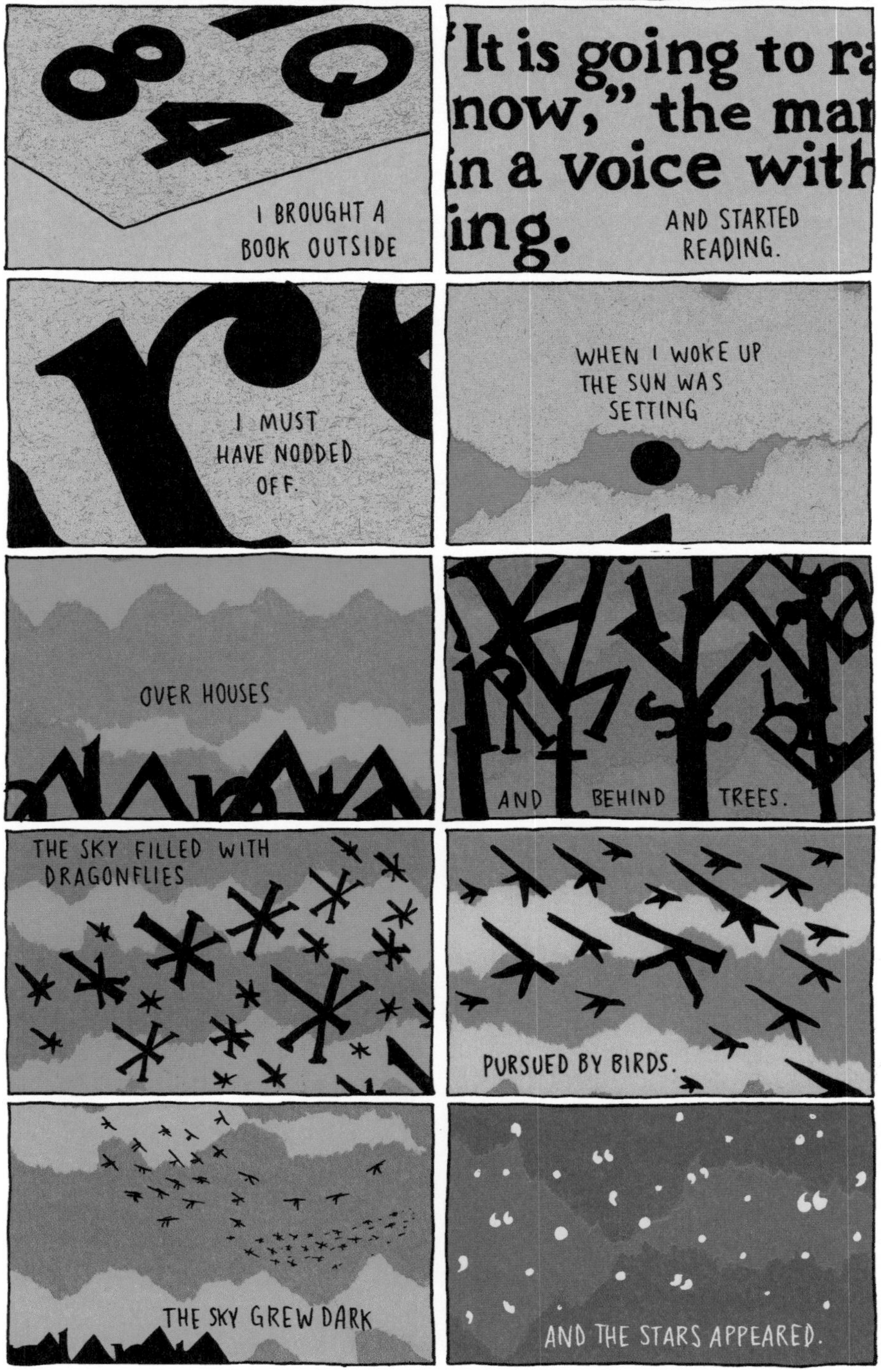

I BROUGHT A BOOK OUTSIDE
"It is going to ra
now," the ma
in a voice with
ing.
AND STARTED READING.
I MUST HAVE NODDED OFF.
WHEN I WOKE UP THE SUN WAS SETTING
OVER HOUSES
AND BEHIND TREES.
THE SKY FILLED WITH DRAGONFLIES
PURSUED BY BIRDS.
THE SKY GREW DARK
AND THE STARS APPEARED.

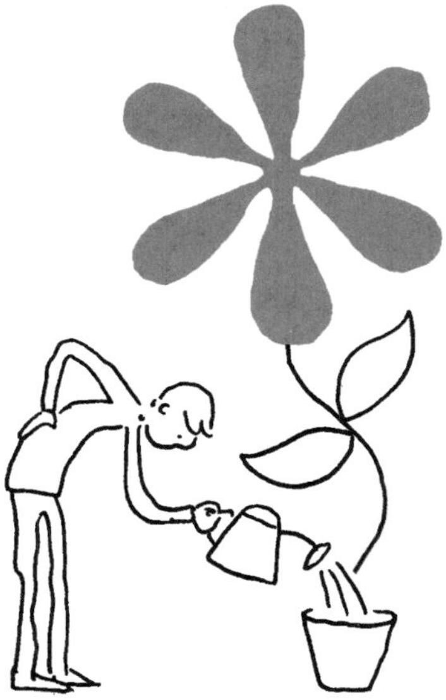

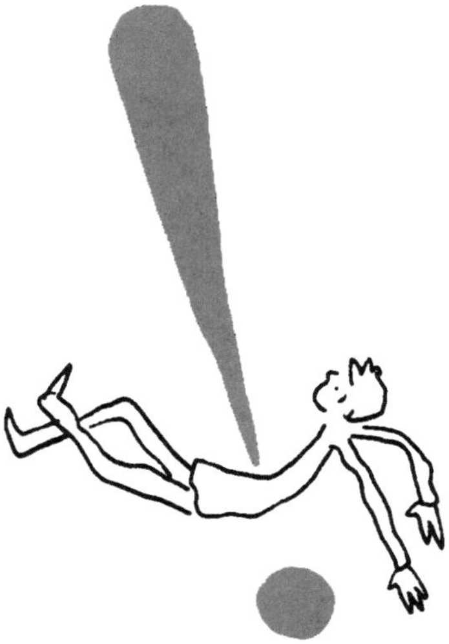

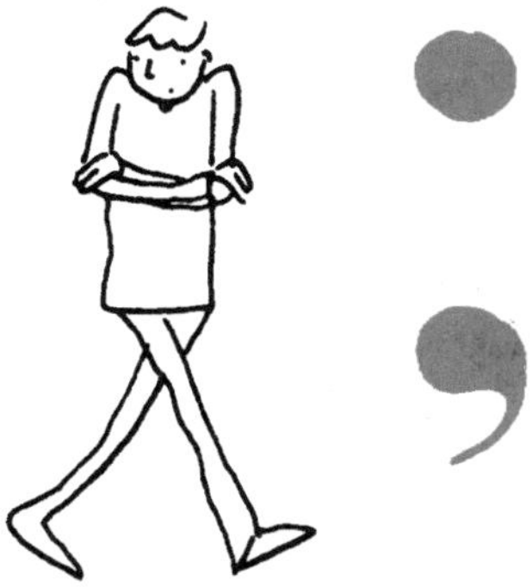

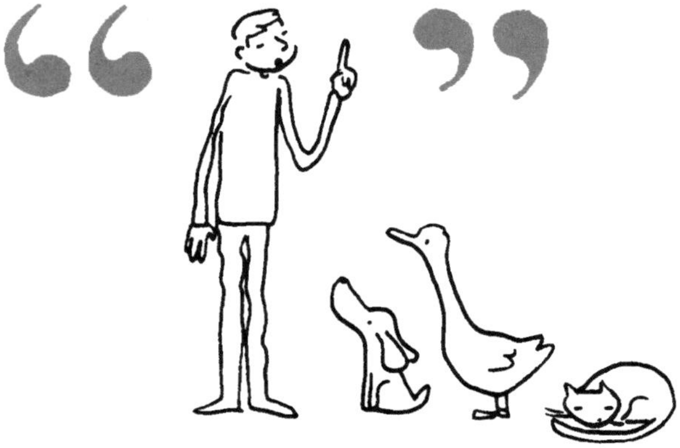

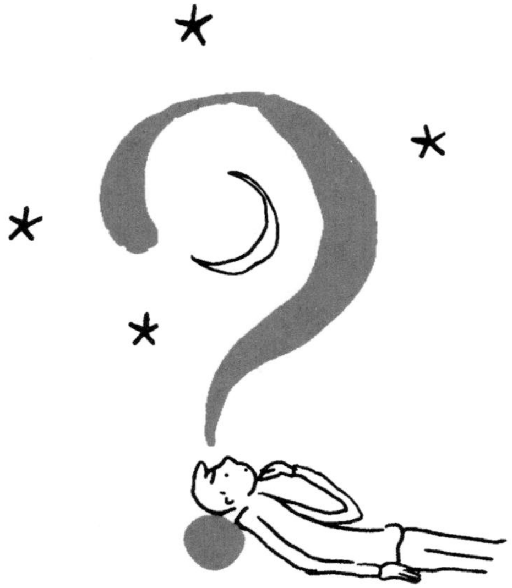

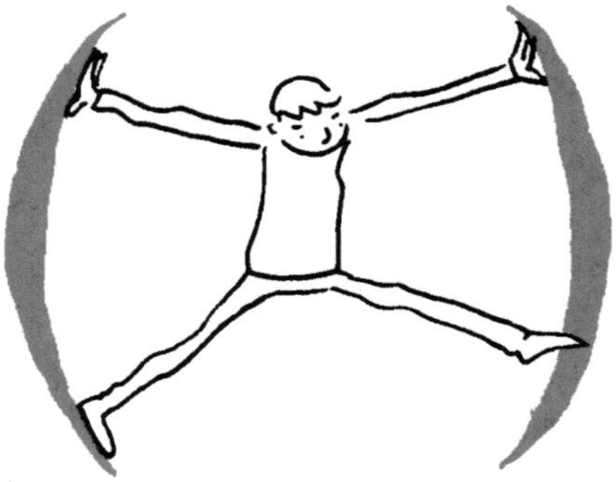

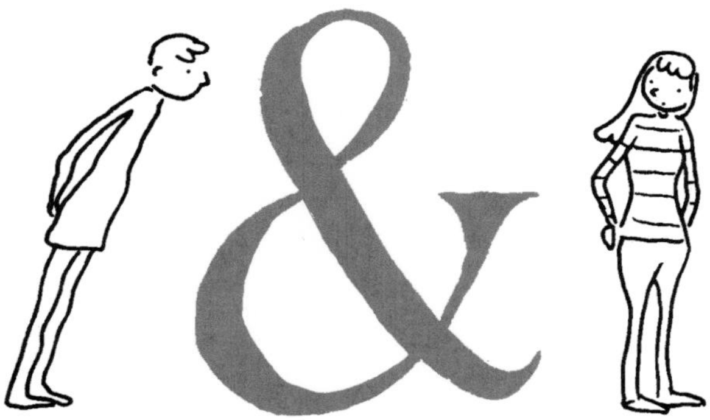

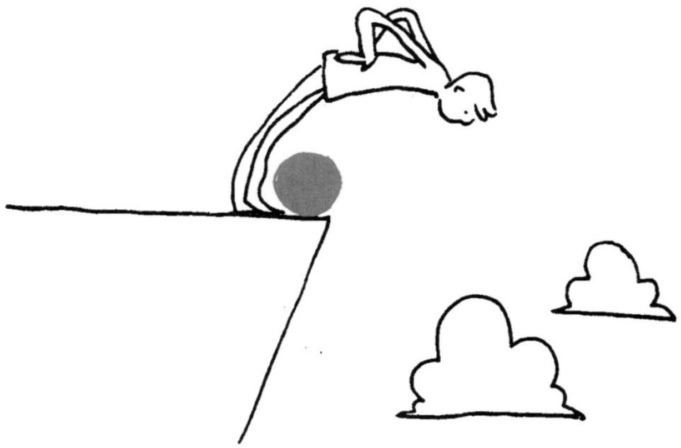

adventures of the ampersand

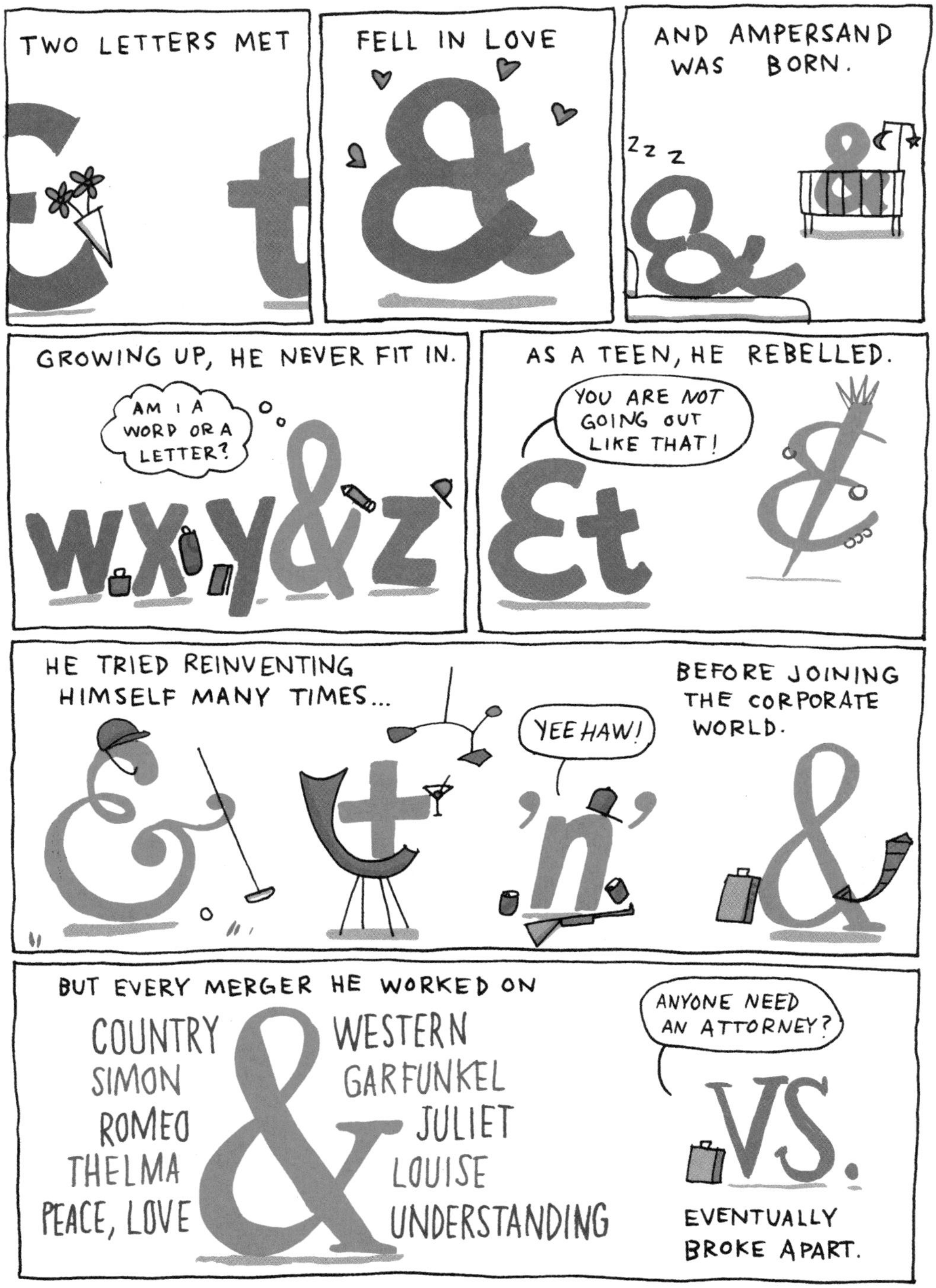
TWO LETTERS MET
FELL IN LOVE
AND AMPERSAND WAS BORN.
Z z z
GROWING UP, HE NEVER FIT IN.
AM I A WORD OR A LETTER?
w x y & z
AS A TEEN, HE REBELLED.
YOU ARE NOT GOING OUT LIKE THAT!
HE TRIED REINVENTING HIMSELF MANY TIMES...
YEE HAW!
BEFORE JOINING THE CORPORATE WORLD.
BUT EVERY MERGER HE WORKED ON
COUNTRY & WESTERN
SIMON & GARFUNKEL
ROMEO & JULIET
THELMA & LOUISE
PEACE, LOVE & UNDERSTANDING
ANYONE NEED AN ATTORNEY?
VS.
EVENTUALLY BROKE APART.

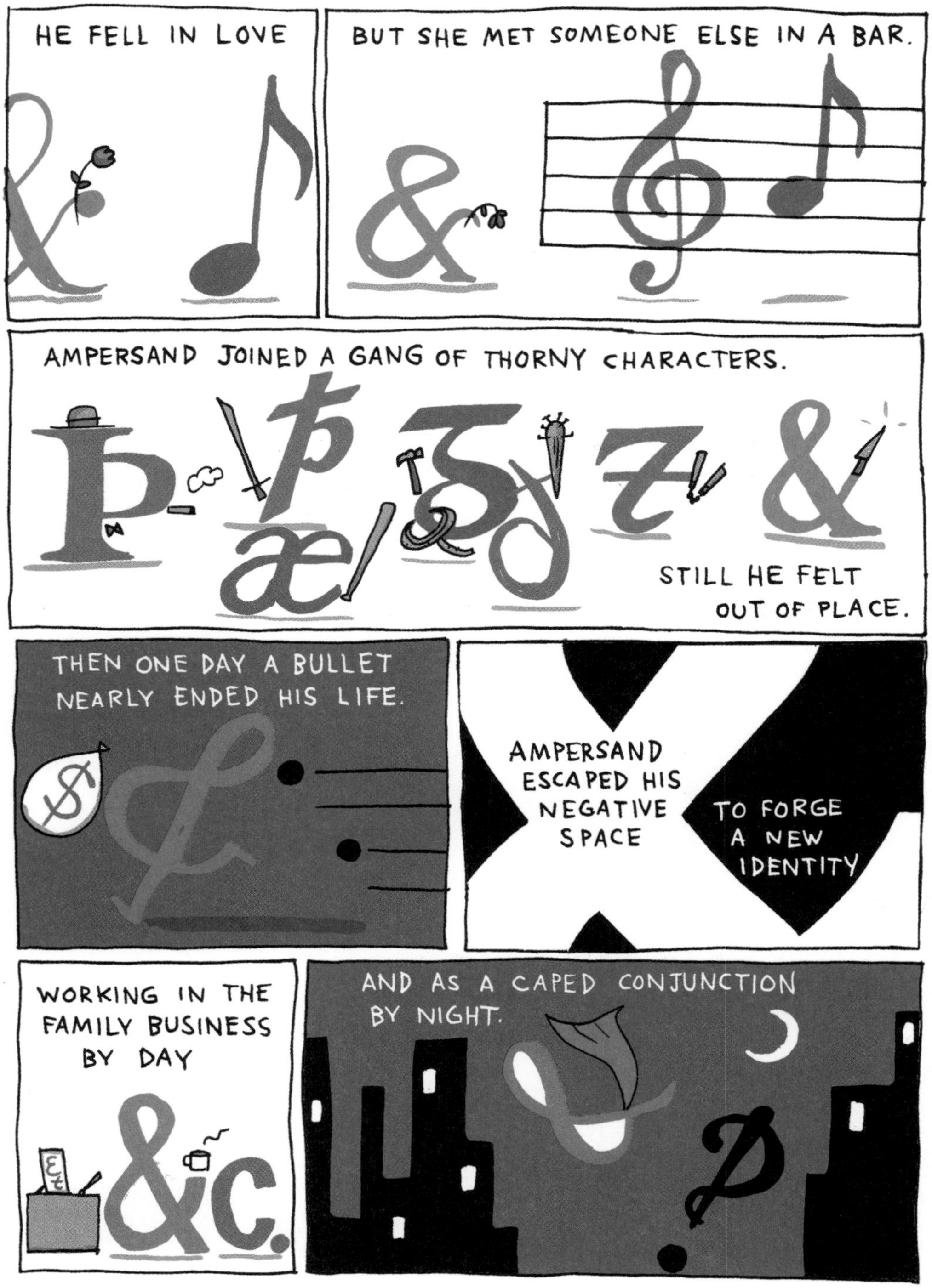
HE FELL IN LOVE
BUT SHE MET SOMEONE ELSE IN A BAR.
AMPERSAND JOINED A GANG OF THORNY CHARACTERS.
STILL HE FELT OUT OF PLACE.
THEN ONE DAY A BULLET NEARLY ENDED HIS LIFE.
AMPERSAND ESCAPED HIS NEGATIVE SPACE
TO FORGE A NEW IDENTITY
WORKING IN THE FAMILY BUSINESS BY DAY
AND AS A CAPED CONJUNCTION BY NIGHT.

I will read
the classics
(someday).

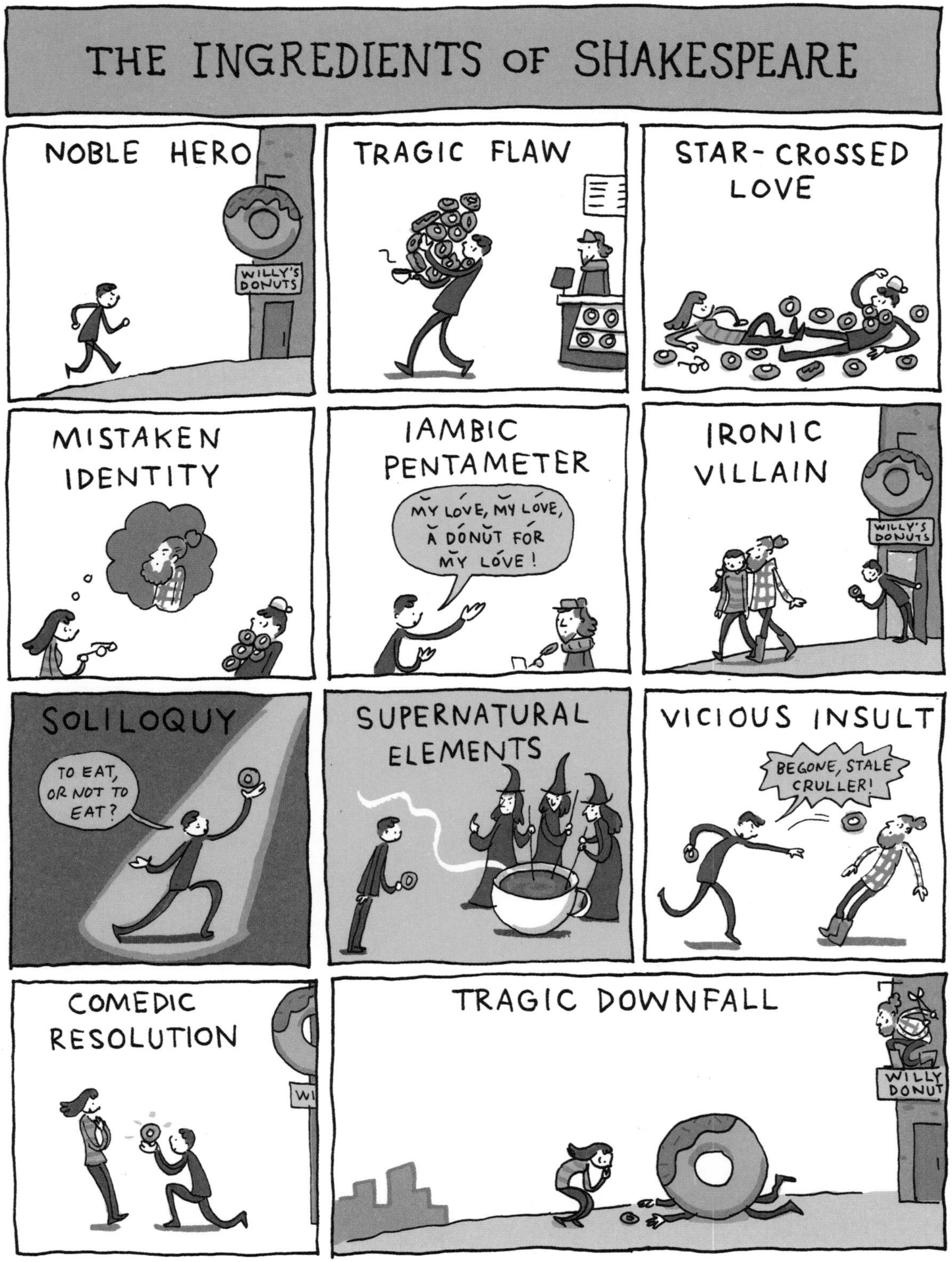
THE INGREDIENTS OF SHAKESPEARE
NOBLE HERO
WILLY'S DONUTS
TRAGIC FLAW
STAR-CROSSED LOVE
MISTAKEN IDENTITY
IAMBIC PENTAMETER
MY LOVE, MY LOVE, A DONUT FOR MY LOVE!
IRONIC VILLAIN
WILLY'S DONUTS
SOLILOQUY
TO EAT, OR NOT TO EAT?
SUPERNATURAL ELEMENTS
VICIOUS INSULT
BEGONE, STALE CRULLER!
COMEDIC RESOLUTION
TRAGIC DOWNFALL

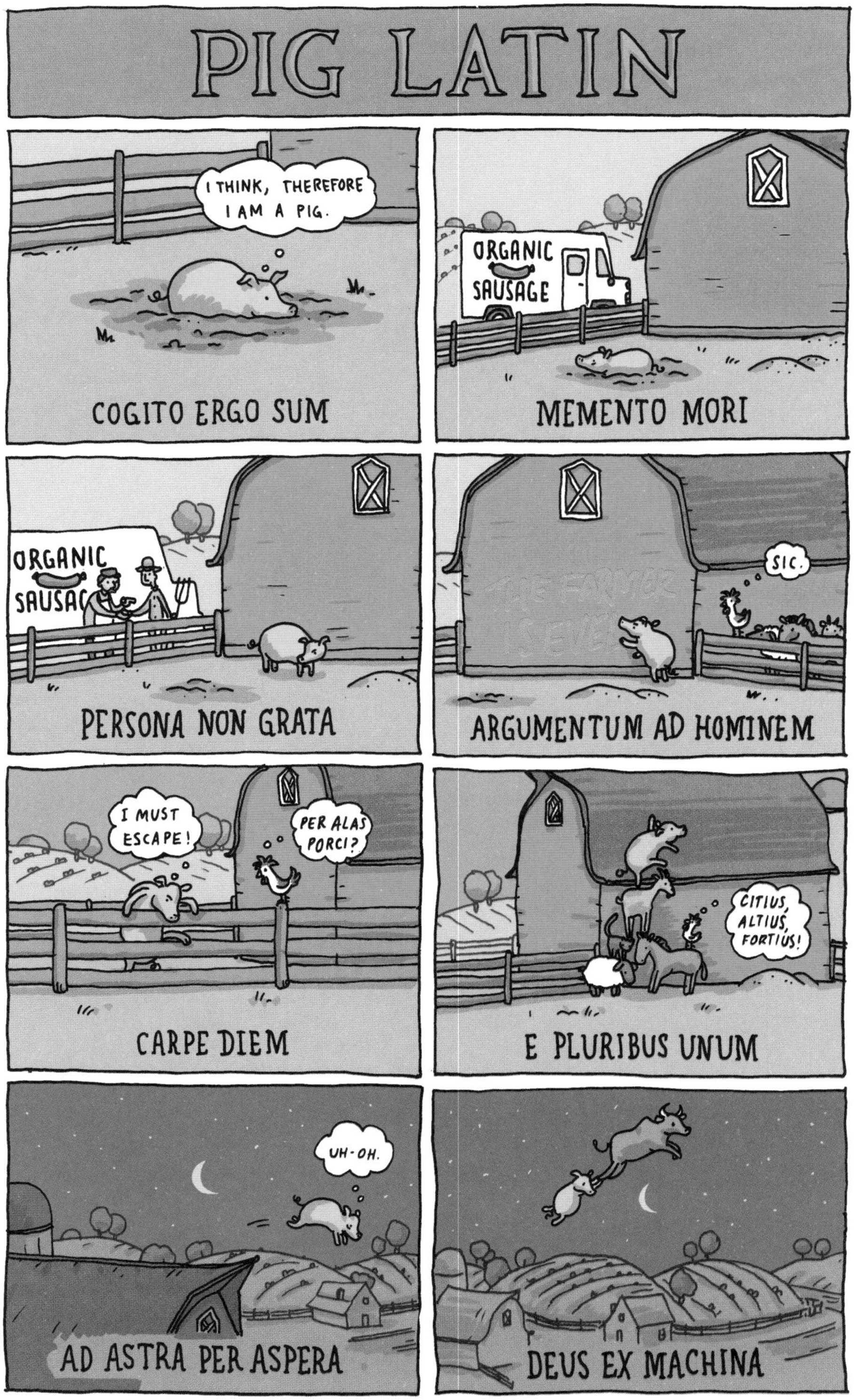
PIG LATIN
I THINK, THEREFORE I AM A PIG.
COGITO ERGO SUM
ORGANIC SAUSAGE
MEMENTO MORI
ORGANIC SAUSAG
PERSONA NON GRATA
SIC.
ARGUMENTUM AD HOMINEM
I MUST ESCAPE!
PER ALAS PORCI?
CARPE DIEM
CITIUS, ALTIUS, FORTIUS!
E PLURIBUS UNUM
UH-OH.
AD ASTRA PER ASPERA
DEUS EX MACHINA

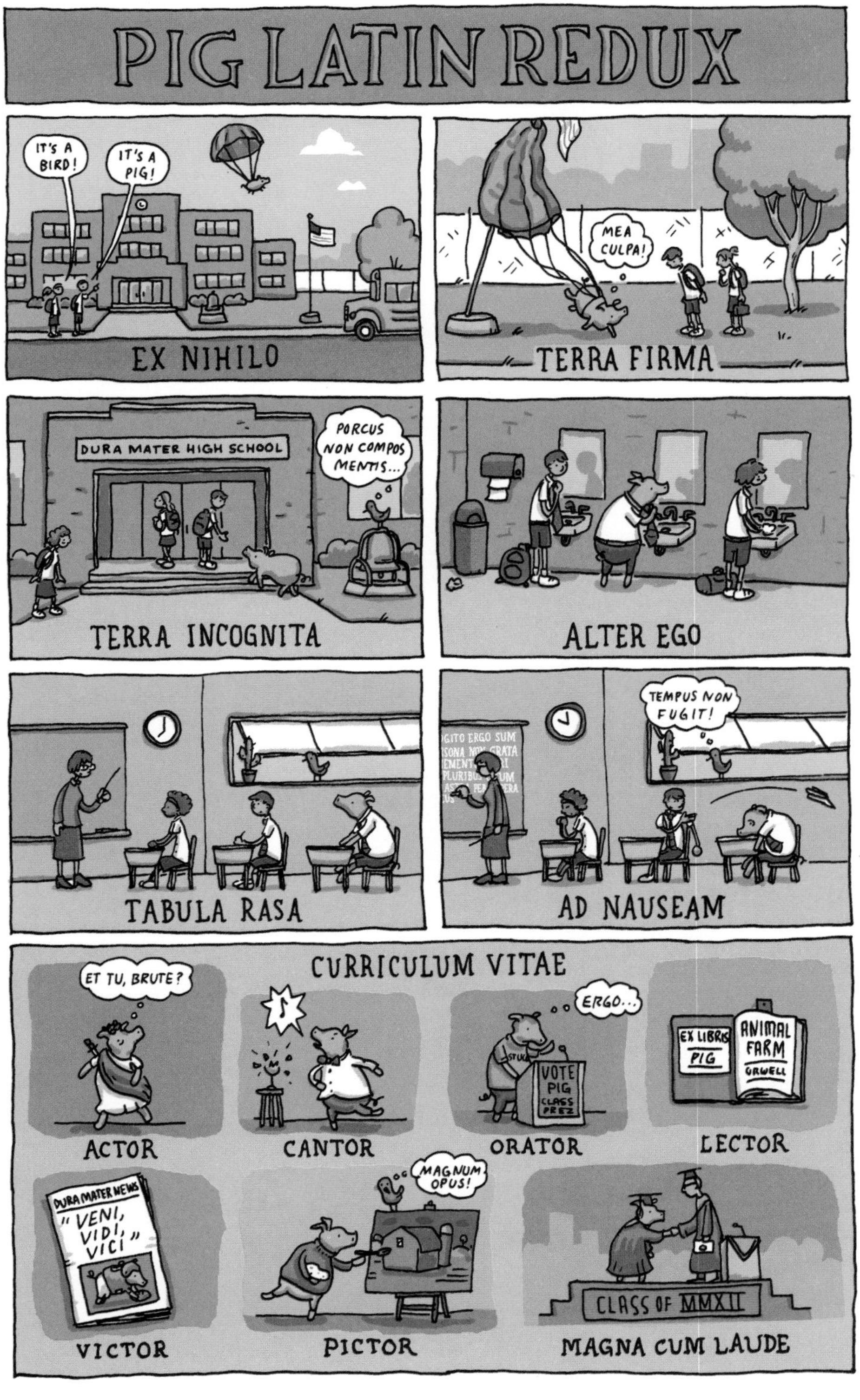
PIG LATIN REDUX
IT'S A BIRD!
IT'S A PIG!
EX NIHILO
MEA CULPA!
TERRA FIRMA
DURA MATER HIGH SCHOOL
PORCUS NON COMPOS MENTIS...
TERRA INCOGNITA
ALTER EGO
TABULA RASA
TEMPUS NON FUGIT!
AD NAUSEAM
CURRICULUM VITAE
ET TU, BRUTE?
ACTOR
CANTOR
ERGO...
VOTE PIG CLASS PREZ
ORATOR
EX LIBRIS PIG
ANIMAL FARM
ORWELL
LECTOR
DURA MATER NEWS
"VENI, VIDI, VICI"
VICTOR
MAGNUM OPUS!
PICTOR
CLASS OF MMXII
MAGNA CUM LAUDE

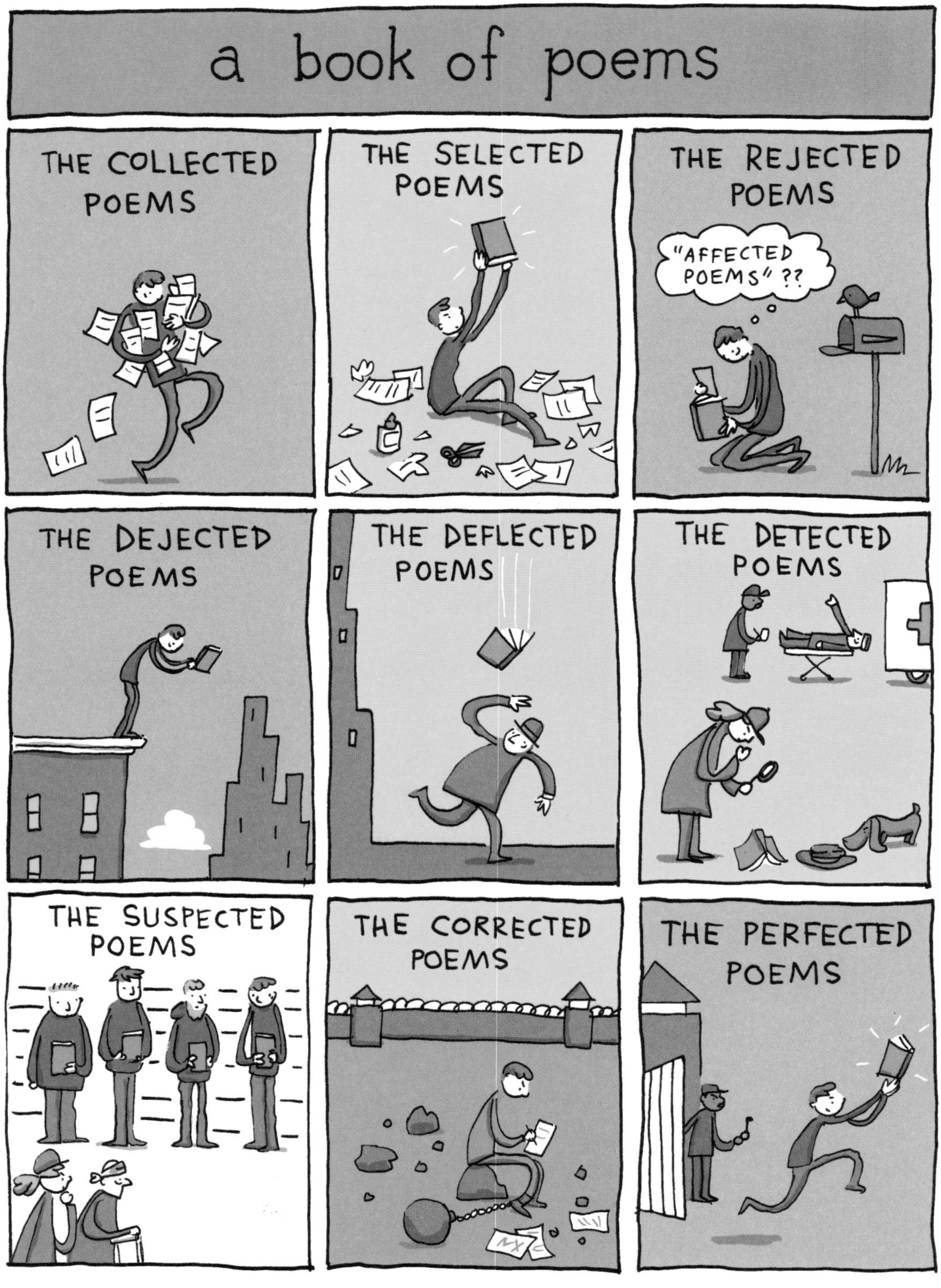
a book of poems
THE COLLECTED POEMS
THE SELECTED POEMS
THE REJECTED POEMS
"AFFECTED POEMS" ??
THE DEJECTED POEMS
THE DEFLECTED POEMS
THE DETECTED POEMS
THE SUSPECTED POEMS
THE CORRECTED POEMS
THE PERFECTED POEMS

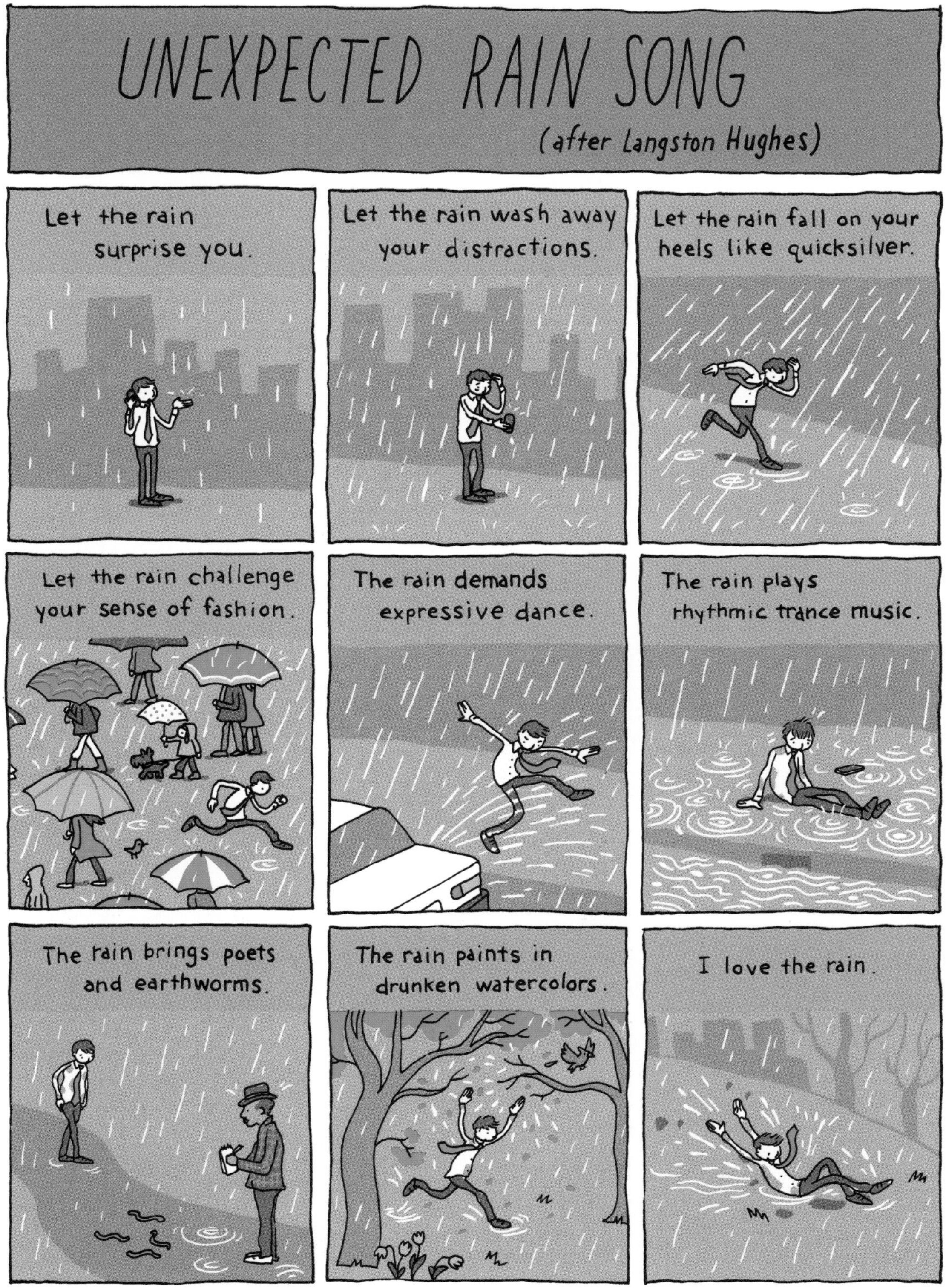
UNEXPECTED RAIN SONG
(after Langston Hughes)
Let the rain surprise you.
Let the rain wash away your distractions.
Let the rain fall on your heels like quicksilver.
Let the rain challenge your sense of fashion.
The rain demands expressive dance.
The rain plays rhythmic trance music.
The rain brings poets and earthworms.
The rain paints in drunken watercolors.
I love the rain.

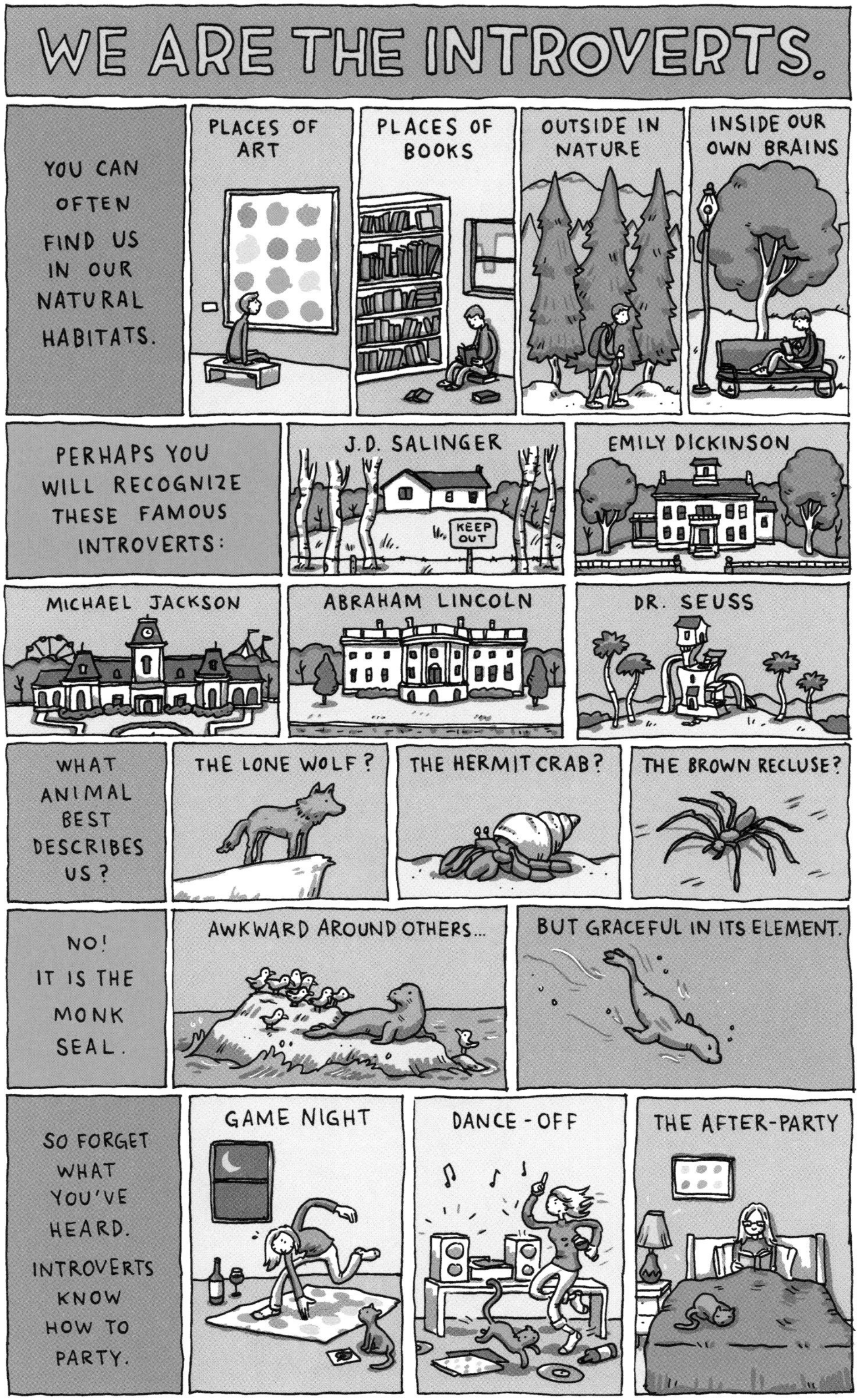
WE ARE THE INTROVERTS.
YOU CAN OFTEN FIND US IN OUR NATURAL HABITATS.
PLACES OF ART
PLACES OF BOOKS
OUTSIDE IN NATURE
INSIDE OUR OWN BRAINS
PERHAPS YOU WILL RECOGNIZE THESE FAMOUS INTROVERTS:
J.D. SALINGER
KEEP OUT
EMILY DICKINSON
MICHAEL JACKSON
ABRAHAM LINCOLN
DR. SEUSS
WHAT ANIMAL BEST DESCRIBES US?
THE LONE WOLF?
THE HERMIT CRAB?
THE BROWN RECLUSE?
NO! IT IS THE MONK SEAL.
AWKWARD AROUND OTHERS...
BUT GRACEFUL IN ITS ELEMENT.
SO FORGET WHAT YOU'VE HEARD. INTROVERTS KNOW HOW TO PARTY.
GAME NIGHT
DANCE-OFF
THE AFTER-PARTY

TYPES OF READERS
PICKY
VORACIOUS
DRAMATIC
TO READ, OR NOT TO READ?
INDECISIVE
OVERPREPARED
UNDERPREPARED
GUILTY
MUST... FINISH...
NOCTURNAL
PHONY
CONTORTIONIST
NEGLECTFUL
RECLUSIVE
KEEP OUT
CAUTION CAUTION
DO NOT DISTURB

DAY JOBS OF THE POETS

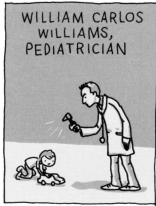

WILLIAM CARLOS WILLIAMS, PEDIATRICIAN

W. B. YEATS, OCCULT MAGICIAN

WALLACE STEVENS, INSURANCE SALESMAN

CHARLES BUKOWSKI, DISGRUNTLED MAILMAN

MAYA ANGELOU, NIGHTCLUB CROONER

HERMAN MELVILLE, ASPIRING HARPOONER

PHILIP LARKIN, PUBLIC LIBRARIAN

ROBERT FROST, FAILED AGRARIAN

T. S. ELIOT, BANK CLERK

JACK KEROUAC, RAILROAD WORK

PABLO NERUDA, DIPLOMAT

EMILY DICKINSON, KEEPER OF CATS

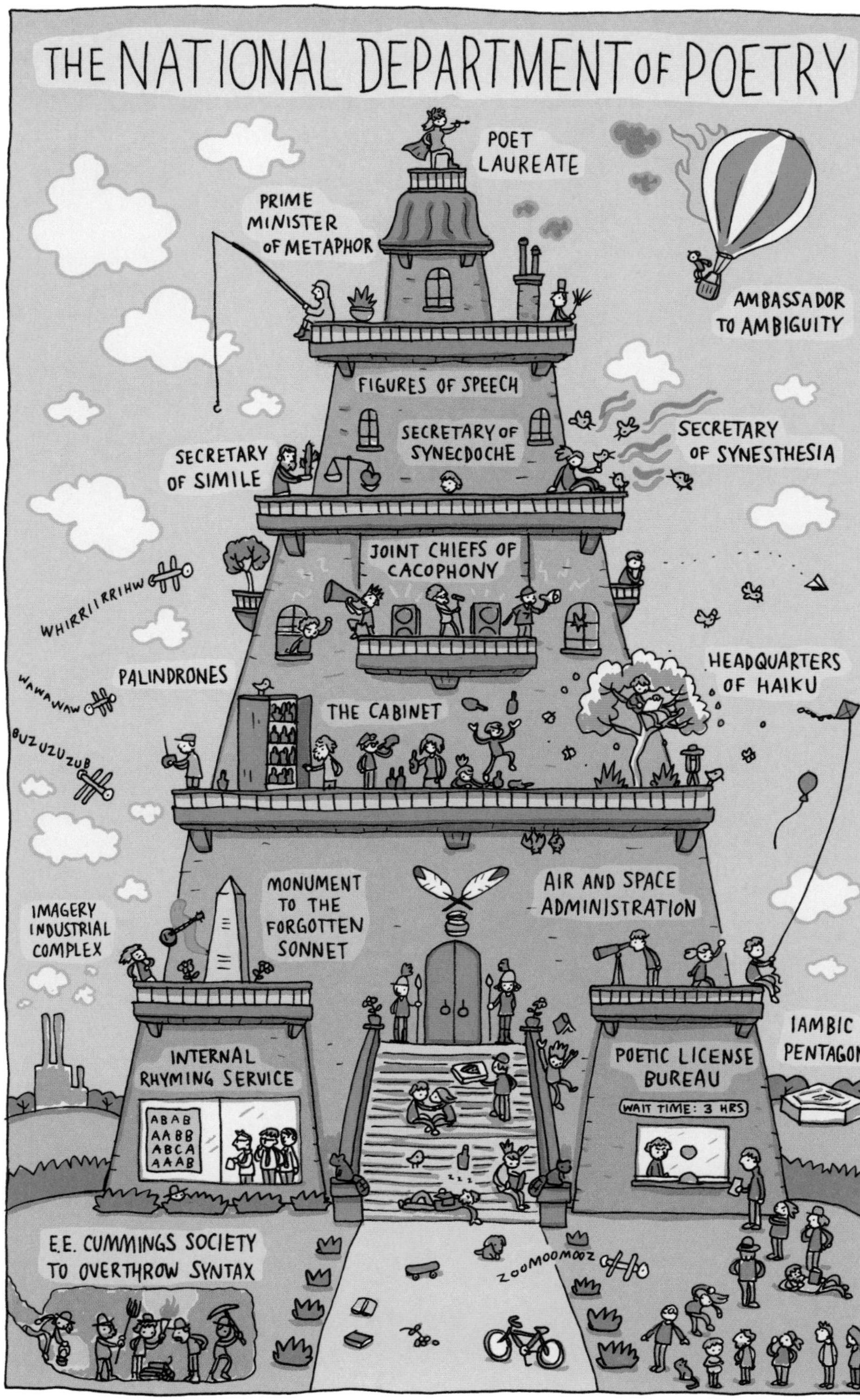
THE NATIONAL DEPARTMENT OF POETRY
POET LAUREATE
PRIME MINISTER OF METAPHOR
AMBASSADOR TO AMBIGUITY
FIGURES OF SPEECH
SECRETARY OF SYNECDOCHE
SECRETARY OF SIMILE
SECRETARY OF SYNESTHESIA
JOINT CHIEFS OF CACOPHONY
WHIRRIIRRIHW
PALINDRONES
WAWAWAW
HEADQUARTERS OF HAIKU
THE CABINET
BUZUZUZUB
MONUMENT TO THE FORGOTTEN SONNET
AIR AND SPACE ADMINISTRATION
IMAGERY INDUSTRIAL COMPLEX
IAMBIC PENTAGON
INTERNAL RHYMING SERVICE
ABAB
AABB
ABCA
AAAB
POETIC LICENSE BUREAU
WAIT TIME: 3 HRS
E.E. CUMMINGS SOCIETY TO OVERTHROW SYNTAX
ZOOMOOMOOZ

I am writing
The Great
American
Novel.

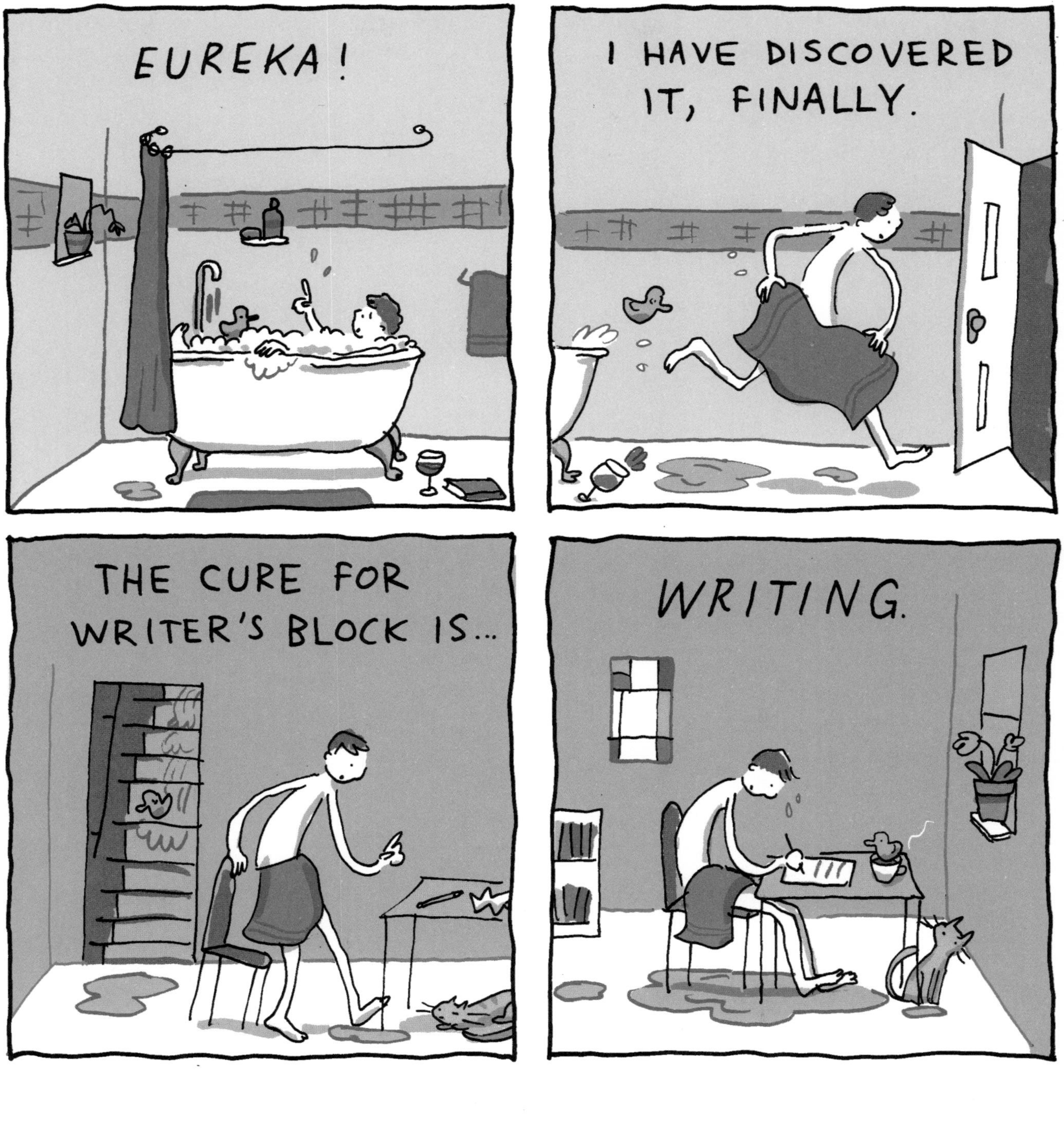
EUREKA!
I HAVE DISCOVERED IT, FINALLY.
THE CURE FOR WRITER'S BLOCK IS...
WRITING.

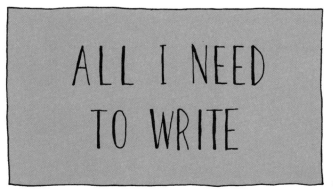

ALL I NEED
TO WRITE

A ROOM WITH A VIEW

NO OTHER WORK TO DO

A CHILDPROOF LOCK

A TICKING CLOCK

NATURAL LIGHT

A CHAIR THAT FITS JUST RIGHT

NEW PAPER AND PENS

SOME ANIMAL FRIENDS

THE RIGHT PHASE OF THE MOON

AMBIENT TUNES

A WORLD OF MY CREATION

OR INTERNAL MOTIVATION.

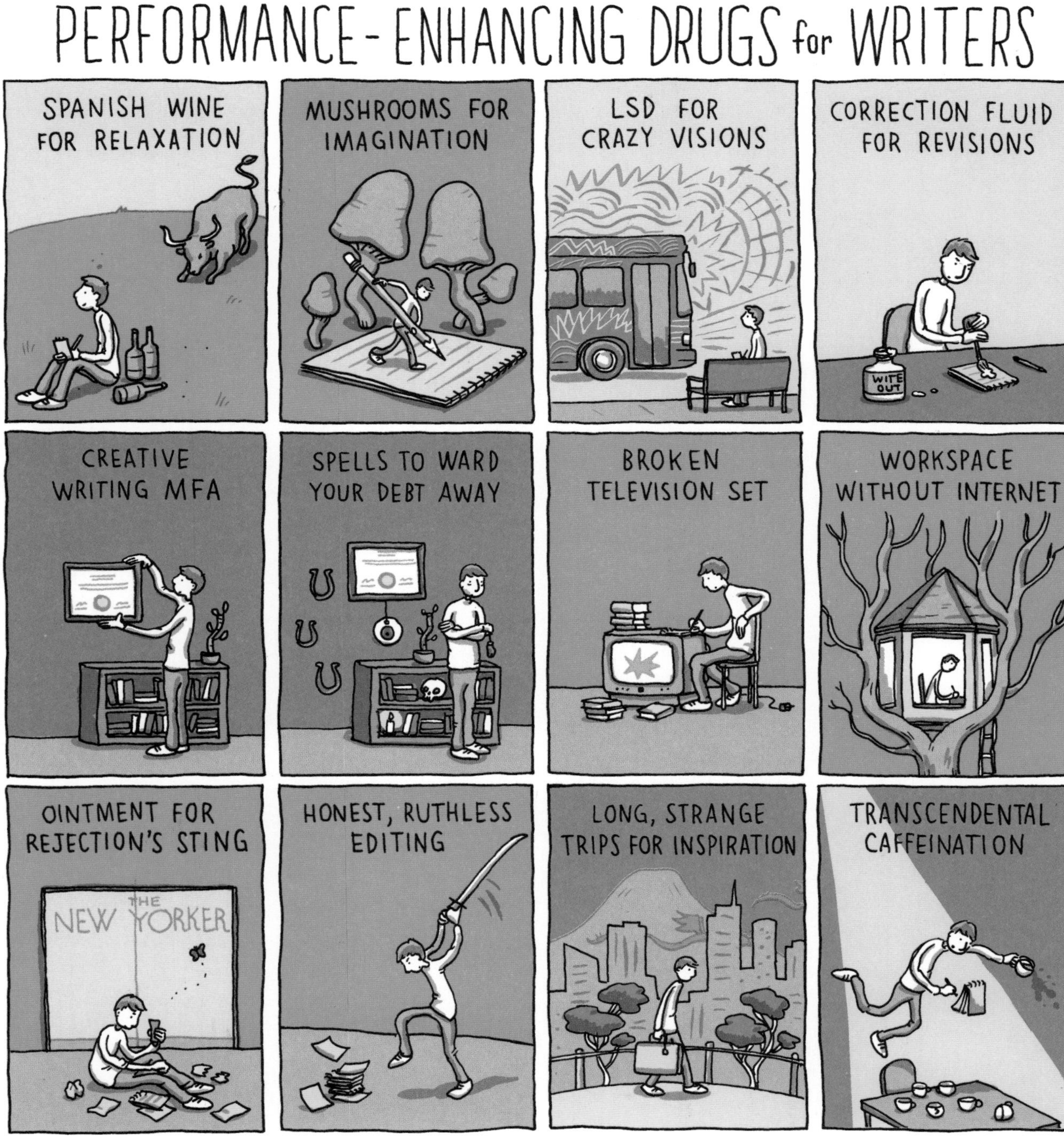
PERFORMANCE-ENHANCING DRUGS for WRITERS
SPANISH WINE FOR RELAXATION
MUSHROOMS FOR IMAGINATION
LSD FOR CRAZY VISIONS
CORRECTION FLUID FOR REVISIONS
WITE OUT
CREATIVE WRITING MFA
SPELLS TO WARD YOUR DEBT AWAY
BROKEN TELEVISION SET
WORKSPACE WITHOUT INTERNET
OINTMENT FOR REJECTION'S STING
THE NEW YORKER
HONEST, RUTHLESS EDITING
LONG, STRANGE TRIPS FOR INSPIRATION
TRANSCENDENTAL CAFFEINATION

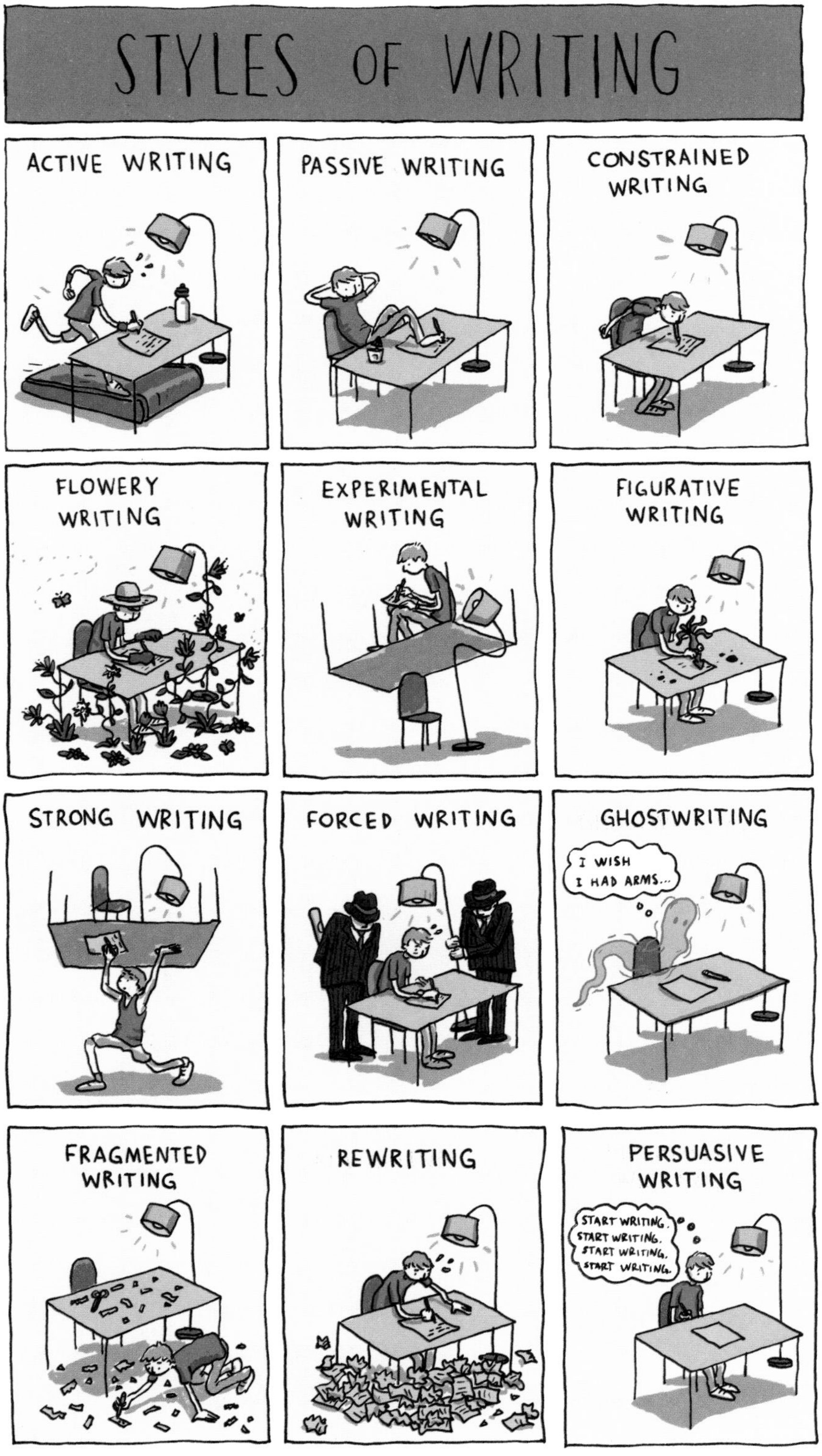
STYLES OF WRITING
ACTIVE WRITING
PASSIVE WRITING
CONSTRAINED WRITING
FLOWERY WRITING
EXPERIMENTAL WRITING
FIGURATIVE WRITING
STRONG WRITING
FORCED WRITING
GHOSTWRITING
I WISH I HAD ARMS...
FRAGMENTED WRITING
REWRITING
PERSUASIVE WRITING
START WRITING. START WRITING. START WRITING. START WRITING.

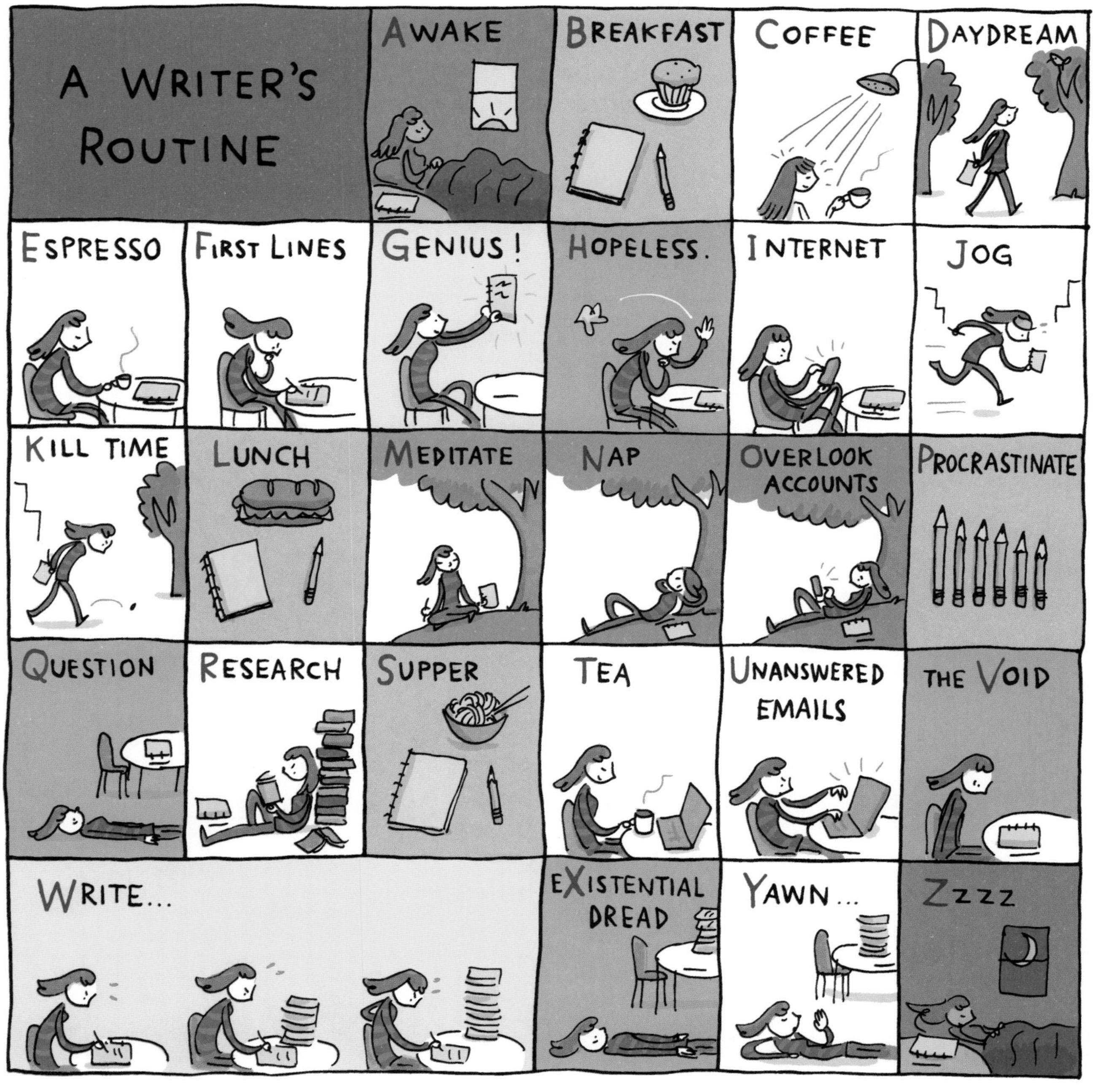
A WRITER'S ROUTINE
AWAKE
BREAKFAST
COFFEE
DAYDREAM
ESPRESSO
FIRST LINES
GENIUS!
HOPELESS.
INTERNET
JOG
KILL TIME
LUNCH
MEDITATE
NAP
OVERLOOK ACCOUNTS
PROCRASTINATE
QUESTION
RESEARCH
SUPPER
TEA
UNANSWERED EMAILS
THE VOID
WRITE...
EXISTENTIAL DREAD
YAWN...
Zzzz

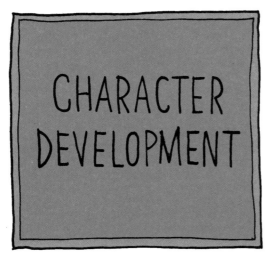

CHARACTER DEVELOPMENT

STOCK CHARACTER

DEVELOPING CHARACTER

WELL-DRAWN CHARACTER

STATIC CHARACTER

DYNAMIC CHARACTER

ROUND CHARACTER

FLAT CHARACTER

SYMPATHETIC CHARACTER

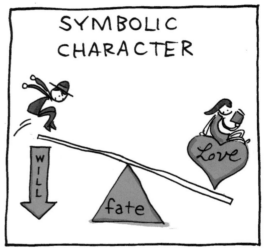

SYMBOLIC CHARACTER

MINOR CHARACTER

MAJOR CHARACTER

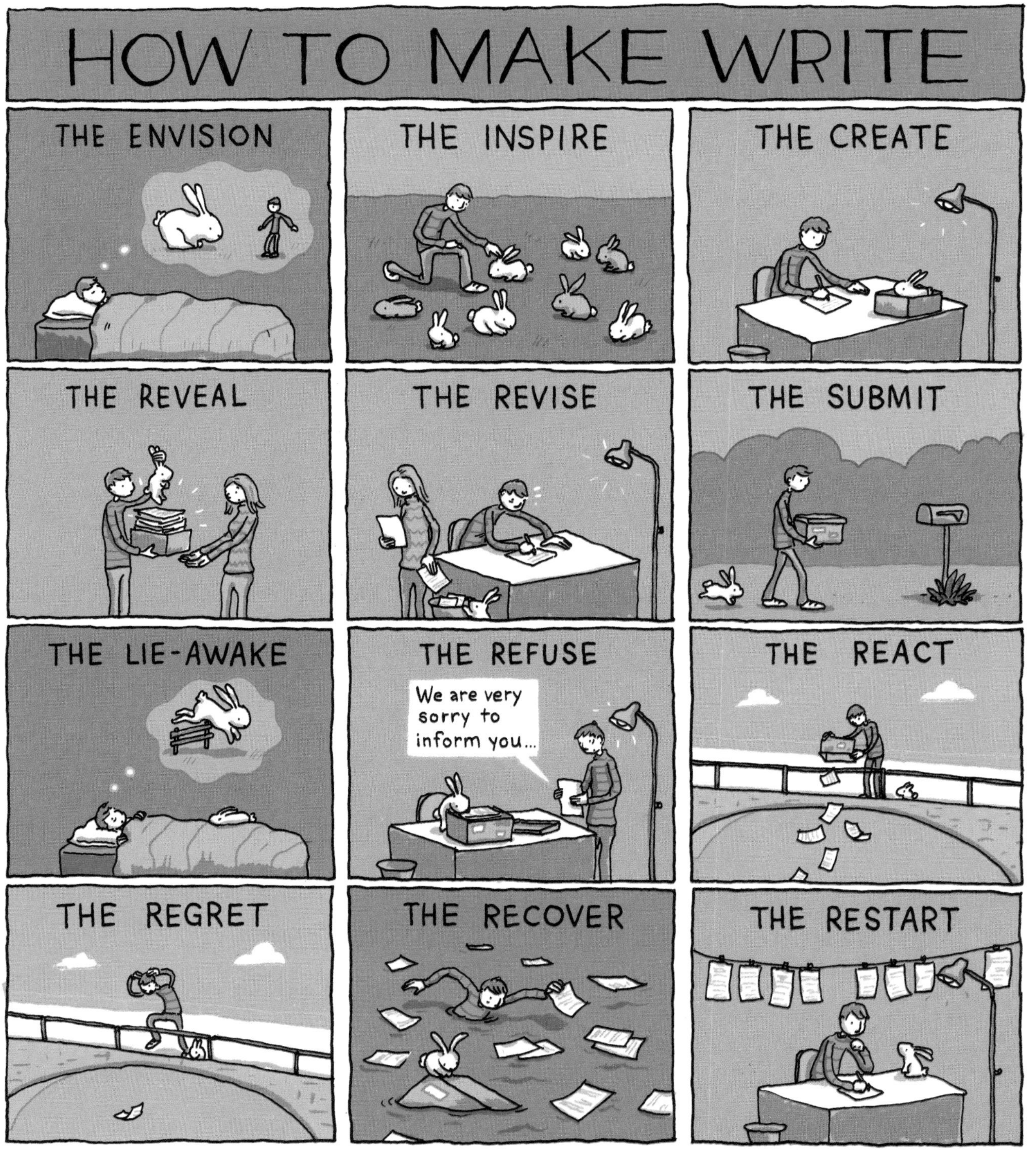
HOW TO MAKE WRITE
THE ENVISION
THE INSPIRE
THE CREATE
THE REVEAL
THE REVISE
THE SUBMIT
THE LIE-AWAKE
THE REFUSE
We are very sorry to inform you...
THE REACT
THE REGRET
THE RECOVER
THE RESTART

BLOCKED

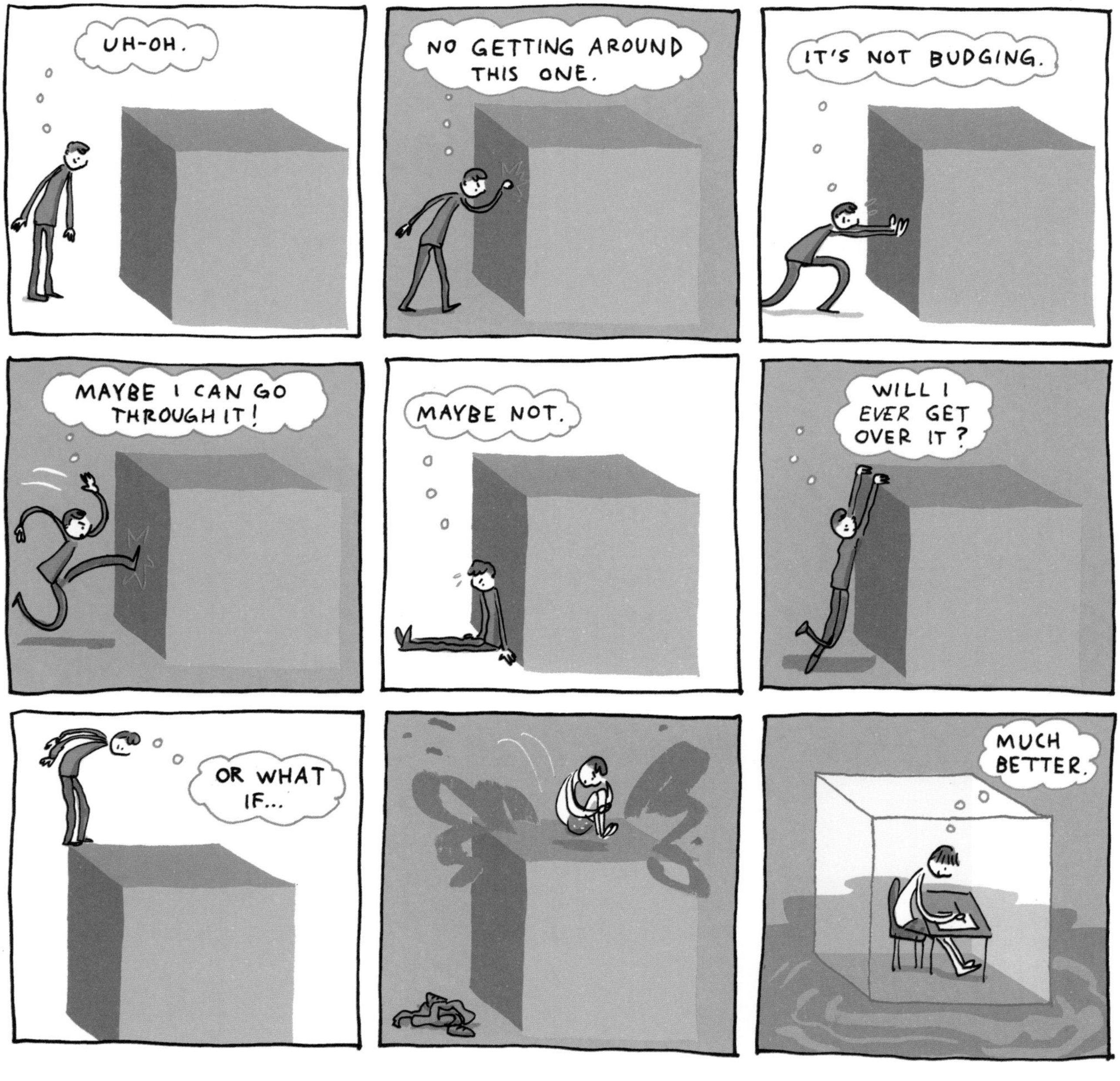

UH-OH.
NO GETTING AROUND THIS ONE.
IT'S NOT BUDGING.
MAYBE I CAN GO THROUGH IT!
MAYBE NOT.
WILL I *EVER* GET OVER IT?
OR WHAT IF...
MUCH BETTER.

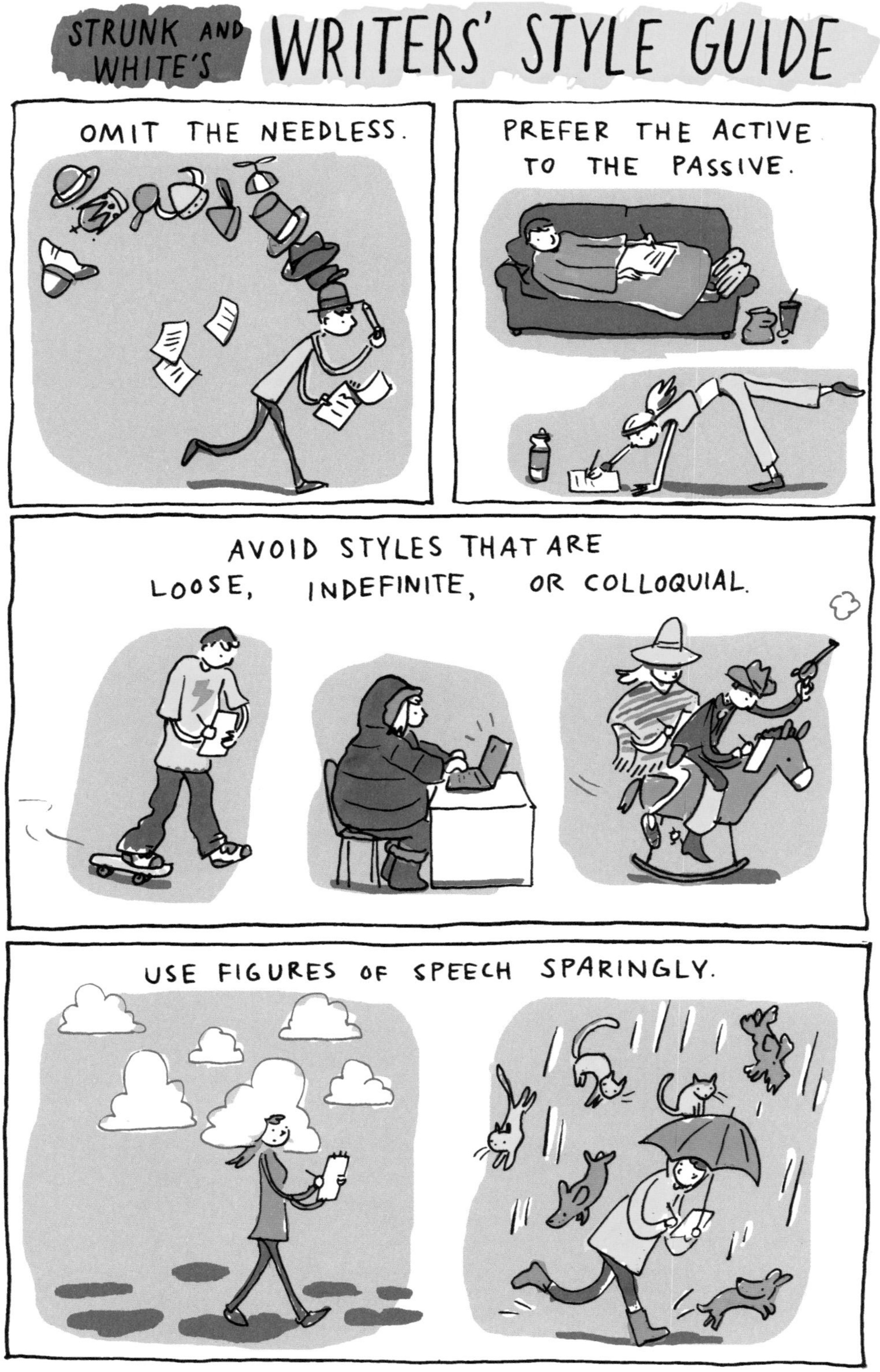
STRUNK AND WHITE'S
WRITERS' STYLE GUIDE
OMIT THE NEEDLESS.
PREFER THE ACTIVE TO THE PASSIVE.
AVOID STYLES THAT ARE LOOSE, INDEFINITE, OR COLLOQUIAL.
USE FIGURES OF SPEECH SPARINGLY.

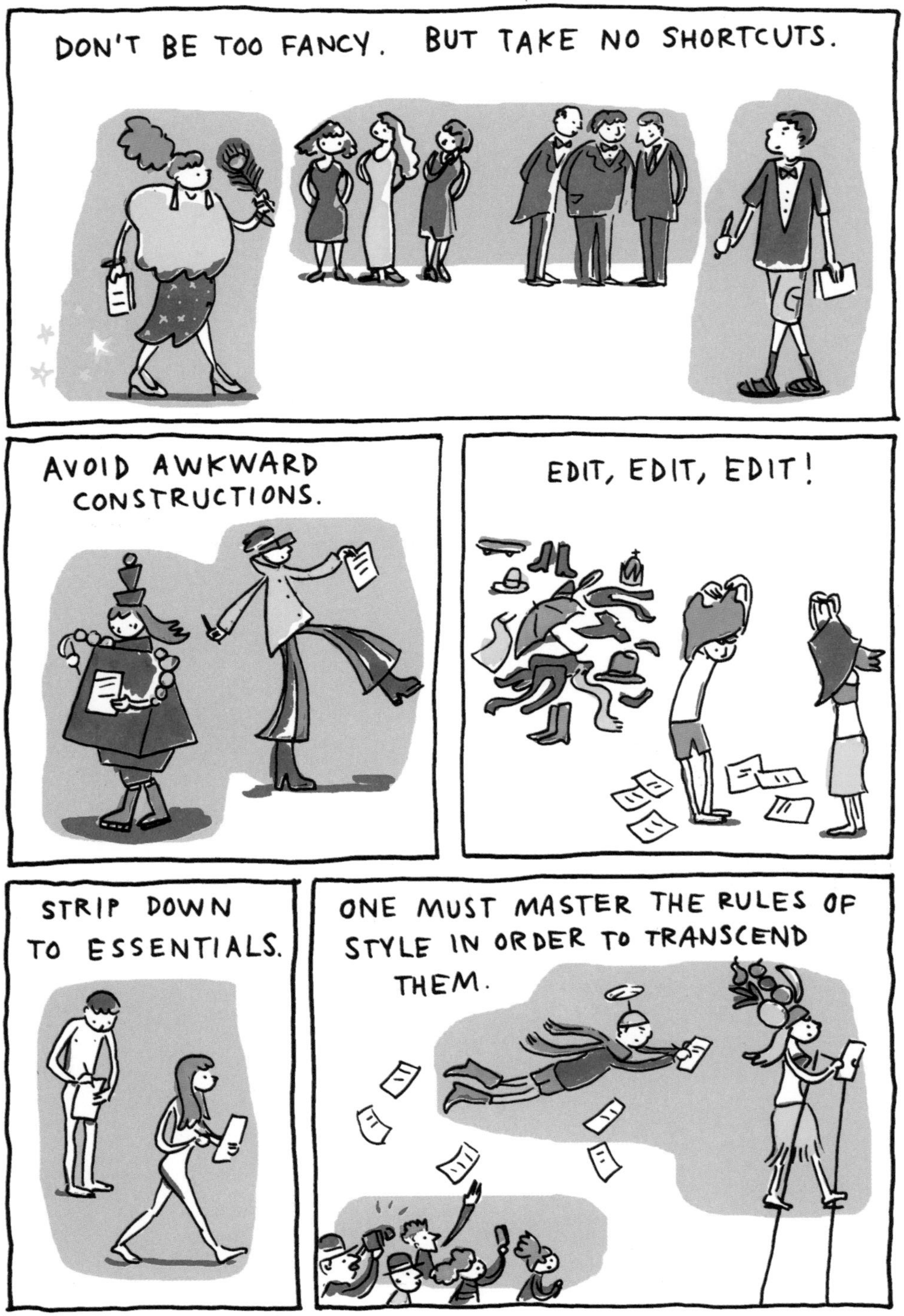

DON'T BE TOO FANCY. BUT TAKE NO SHORTCUTS.
AVOID AWKWARD CONSTRUCTIONS.
EDIT, EDIT, EDIT!
STRIP DOWN TO ESSENTIALS.
ONE MUST MASTER THE RULES OF STYLE IN ORDER TO TRANSCEND THEM.

I carry
a notebook
with me at
all times.

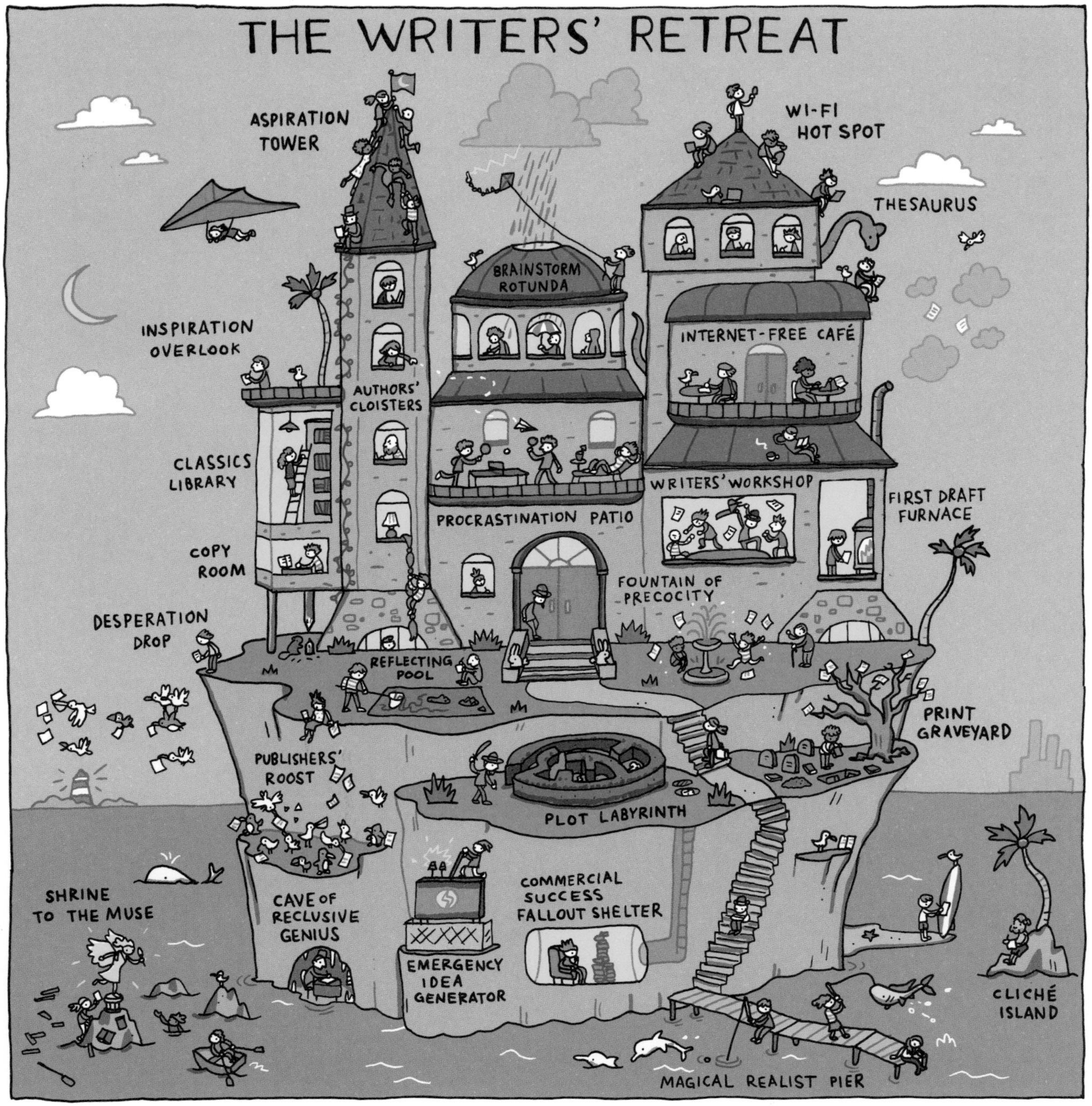
THE WRITERS' RETREAT
ASPIRATION TOWER
WI-FI HOT SPOT
THESAURUS
BRAINSTORM ROTUNDA
INSPIRATION OVERLOOK
INTERNET-FREE CAFÉ
AUTHORS' CLOISTERS
CLASSICS LIBRARY
WRITERS' WORKSHOP
FIRST DRAFT FURNACE
PROCRASTINATION PATIO
COPY ROOM
FOUNTAIN OF PRECOCITY
DESPERATION DROP
REFLECTING POOL
PRINT GRAVEYARD
PUBLISHERS' ROOST
PLOT LABYRINTH
SHRINE TO THE MUSE
CAVE OF RECLUSIVE GENIUS
COMMERCIAL SUCCESS FALLOUT SHELTER
EMERGENCY IDEA GENERATOR
CLICHÉ ISLAND
MAGICAL REALIST PIER

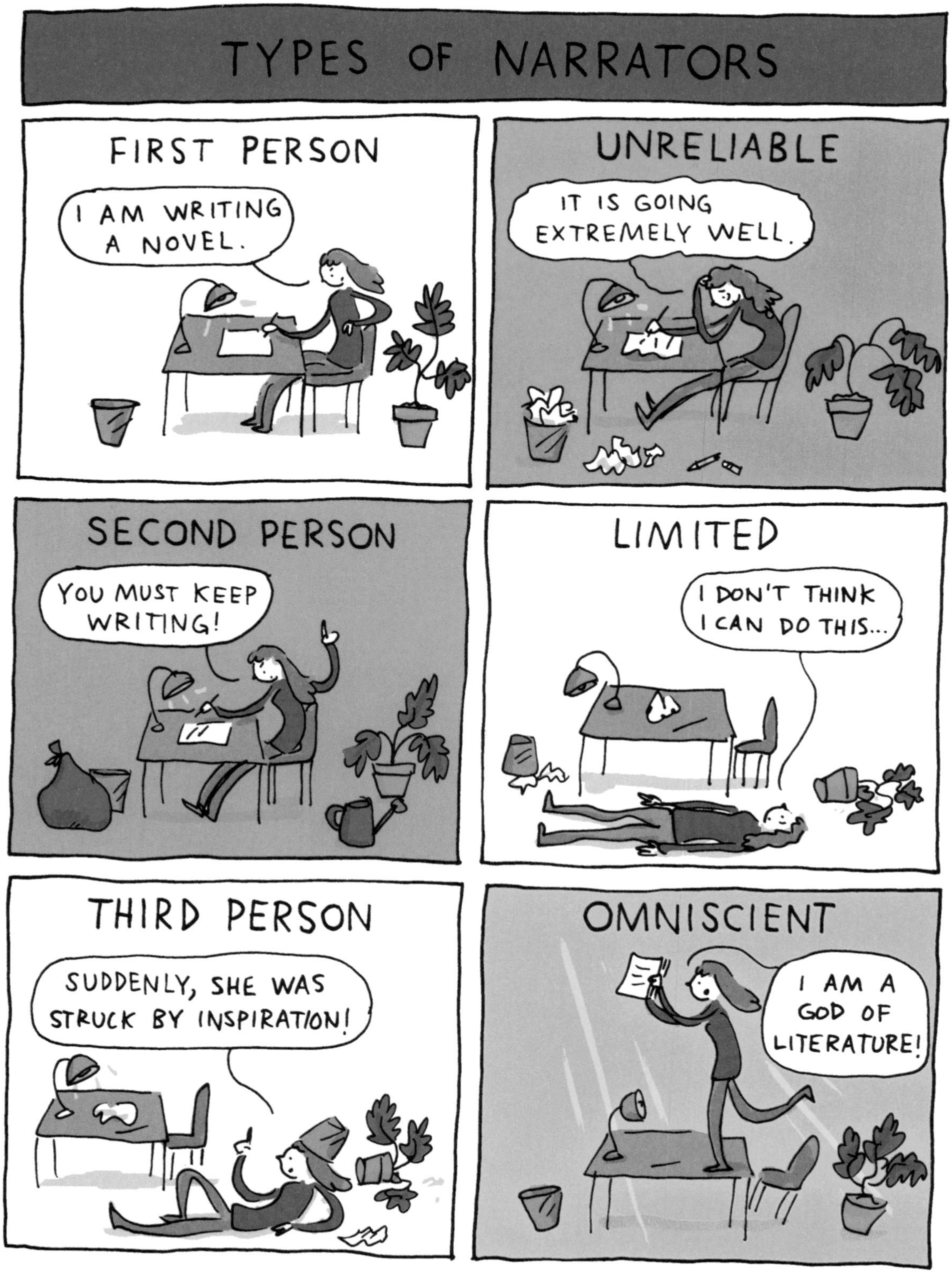
TYPES OF NARRATORS
FIRST PERSON
I AM WRITING A NOVEL.
UNRELIABLE
IT IS GOING EXTREMELY WELL.
SECOND PERSON
YOU MUST KEEP WRITING!
LIMITED
I DON'T THINK I CAN DO THIS...
THIRD PERSON
SUDDENLY, SHE WAS STRUCK BY INSPIRATION!
OMNISCIENT
I AM A GOD OF LITERATURE!

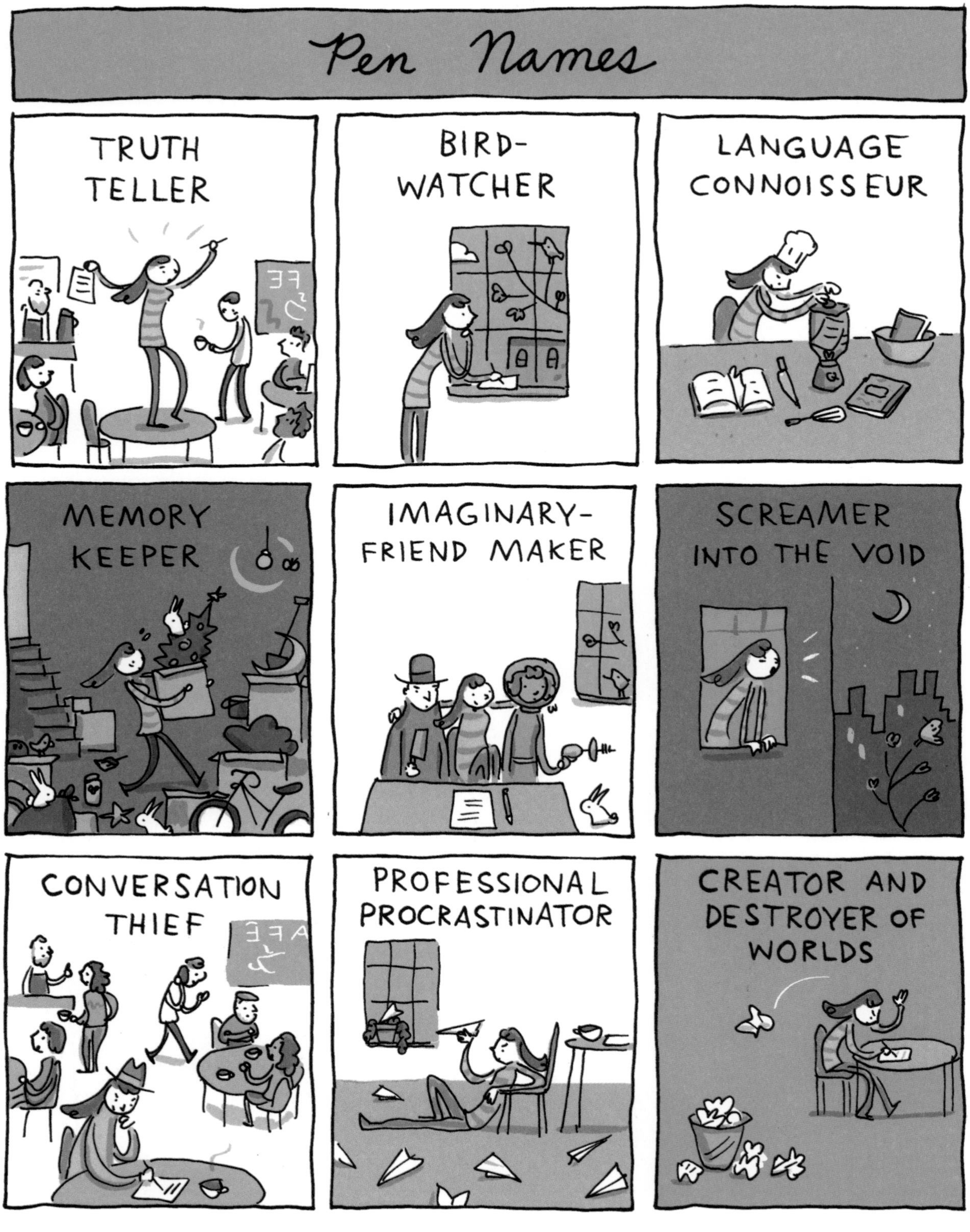
Pen Names
TRUTH TELLER
BIRD-WATCHER
LANGUAGE CONNOISSEUR
MEMORY KEEPER
IMAGINARY-FRIEND MAKER
SCREAMER INTO THE VOID
CONVERSATION THIEF
PROFESSIONAL PROCRASTINATOR
CREATOR AND DESTROYER OF WORLDS

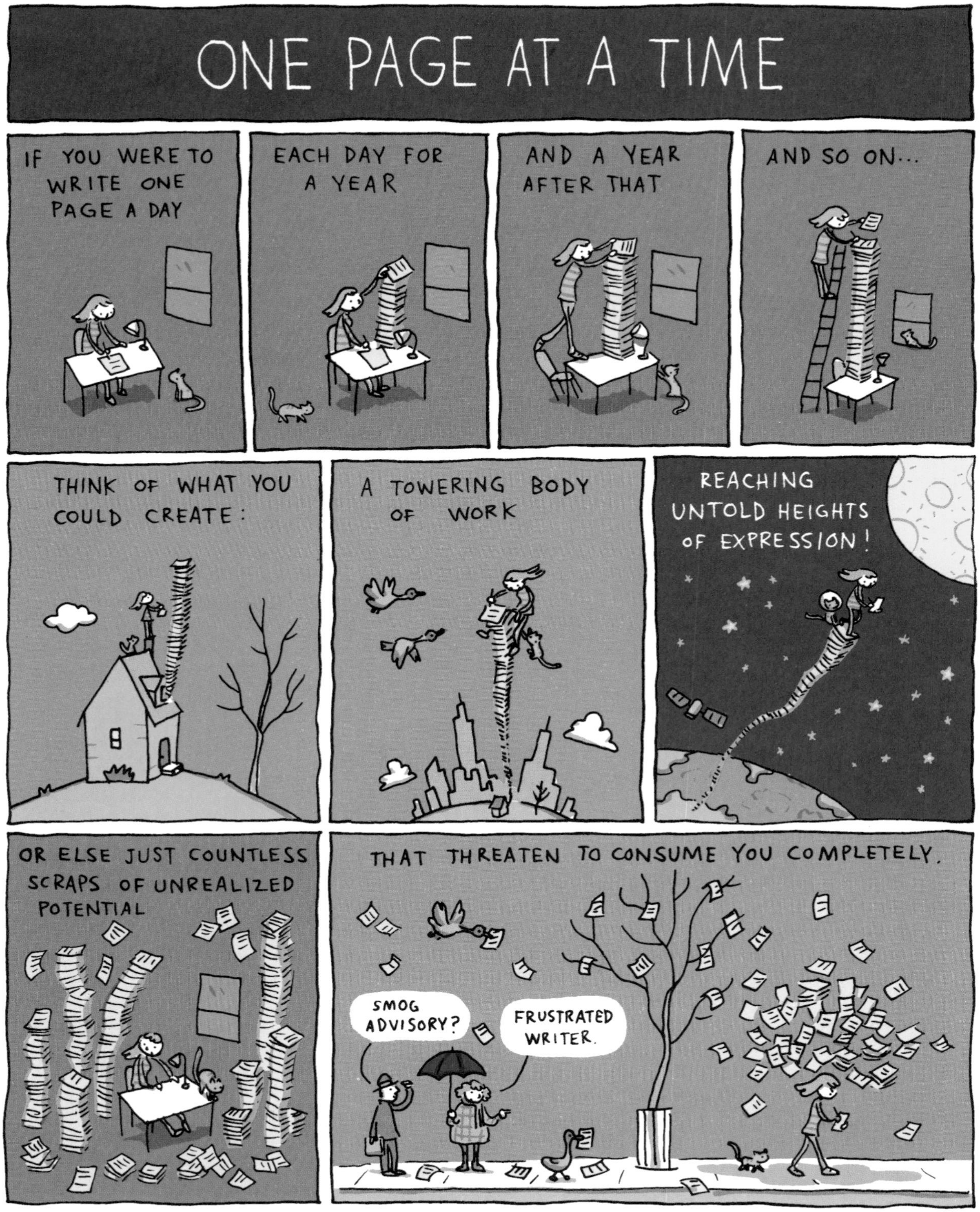
ONE PAGE AT A TIME
IF YOU WERE TO WRITE ONE PAGE A DAY
EACH DAY FOR A YEAR
AND A YEAR AFTER THAT
AND SO ON...
THINK OF WHAT YOU COULD CREATE:
A TOWERING BODY OF WORK
REACHING UNTOLD HEIGHTS OF EXPRESSION!
OR ELSE JUST COUNTLESS SCRAPS OF UNREALIZED POTENTIAL
THAT THREATEN TO CONSUME YOU COMPLETELY.
SMOG ADVISORY?
FRUSTRATED WRITER.

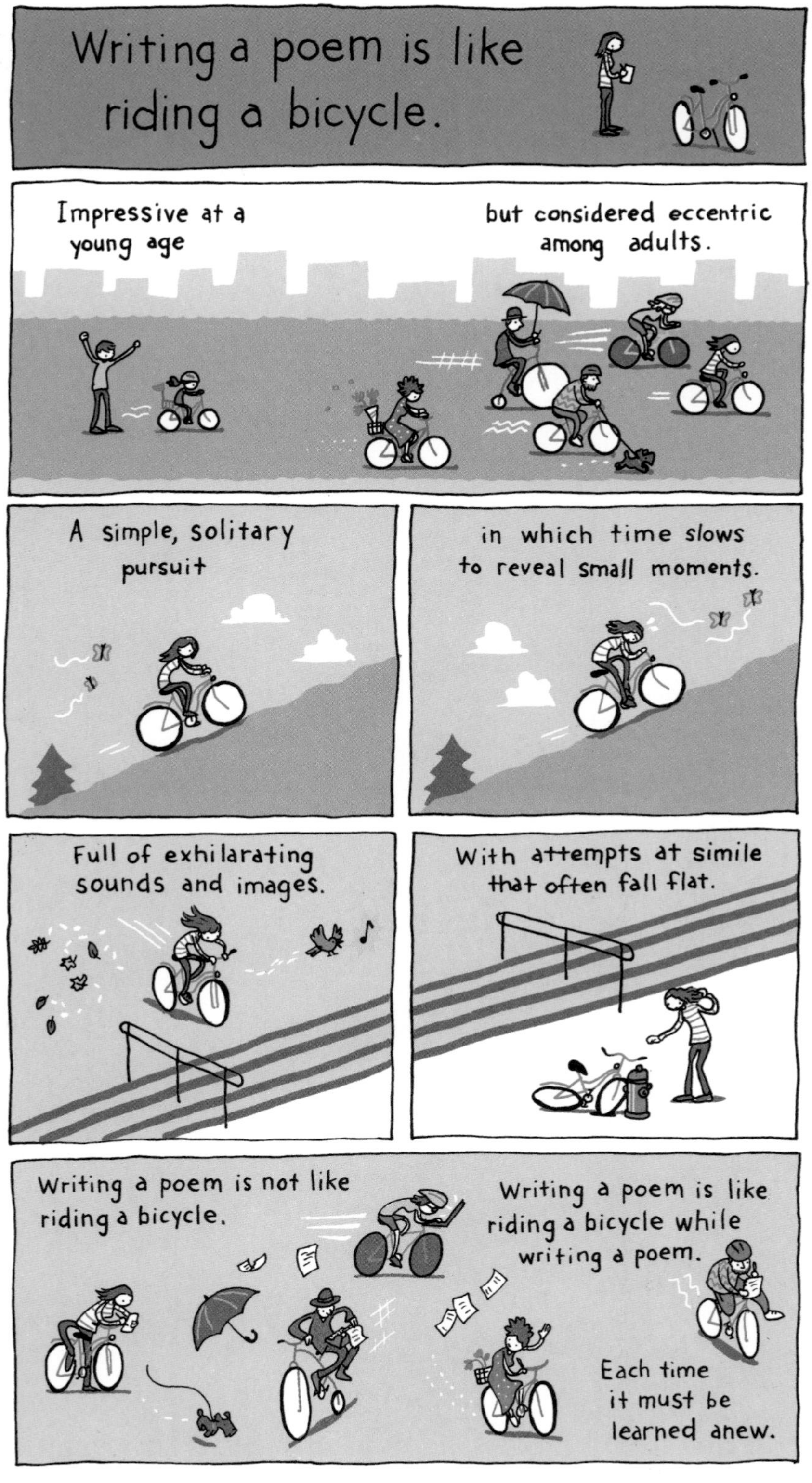

Writing a poem is like riding a bicycle.
Impressive at a young age
but considered eccentric among adults.
A simple, solitary pursuit
in which time slows to reveal small moments.
Full of exhilarating sounds and images.
With attempts at simile that often fall flat.
Writing a poem is not like riding a bicycle.
Writing a poem is like riding a bicycle while writing a poem.
Each time it must be learned anew.

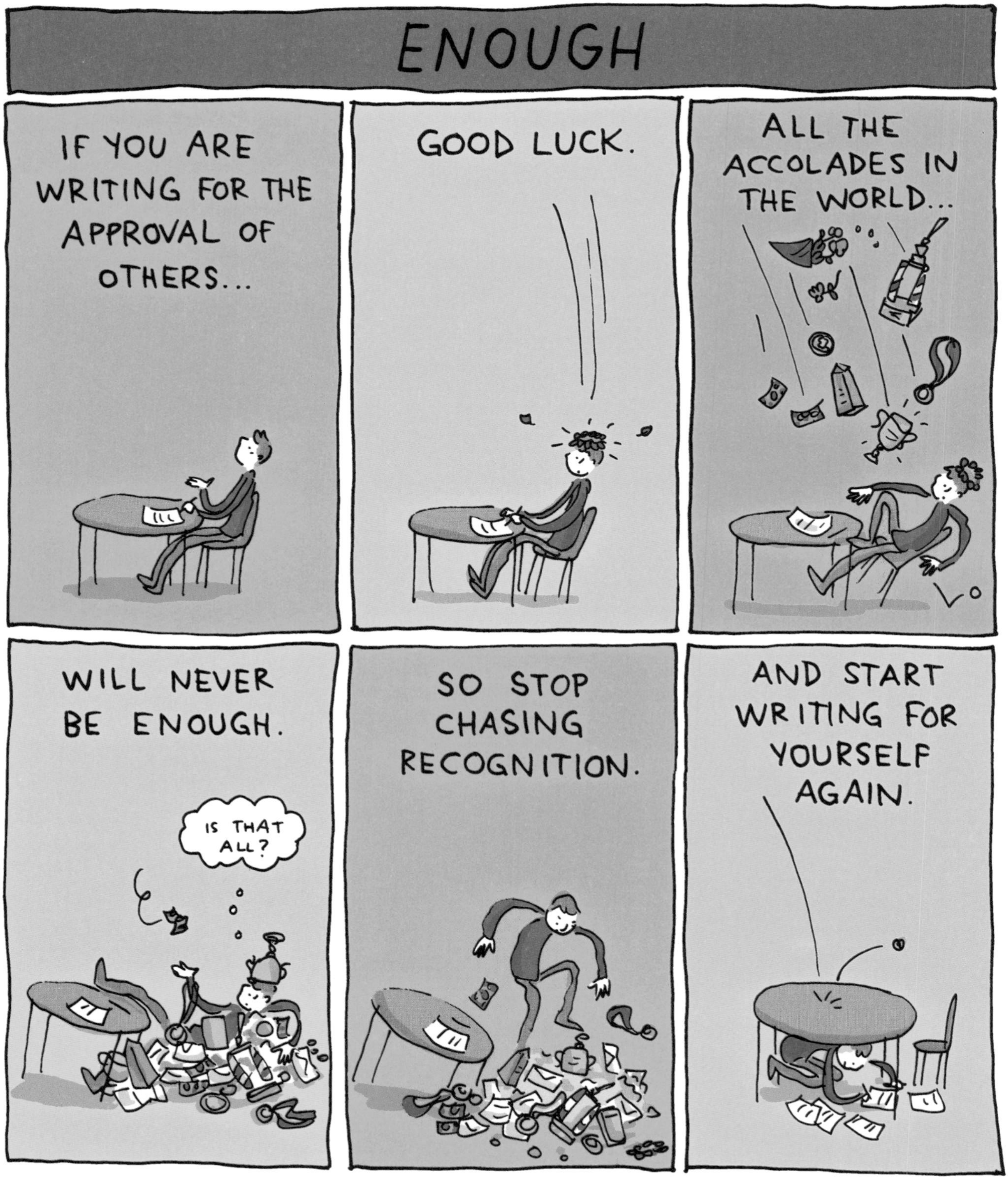
ENOUGH
IF YOU ARE WRITING FOR THE APPROVAL OF OTHERS...
GOOD LUCK.
ALL THE ACCOLADES IN THE WORLD...
WILL NEVER BE ENOUGH.
IS THAT ALL?
SO STOP CHASING RECOGNITION.
AND START WRITING FOR YOURSELF AGAIN.

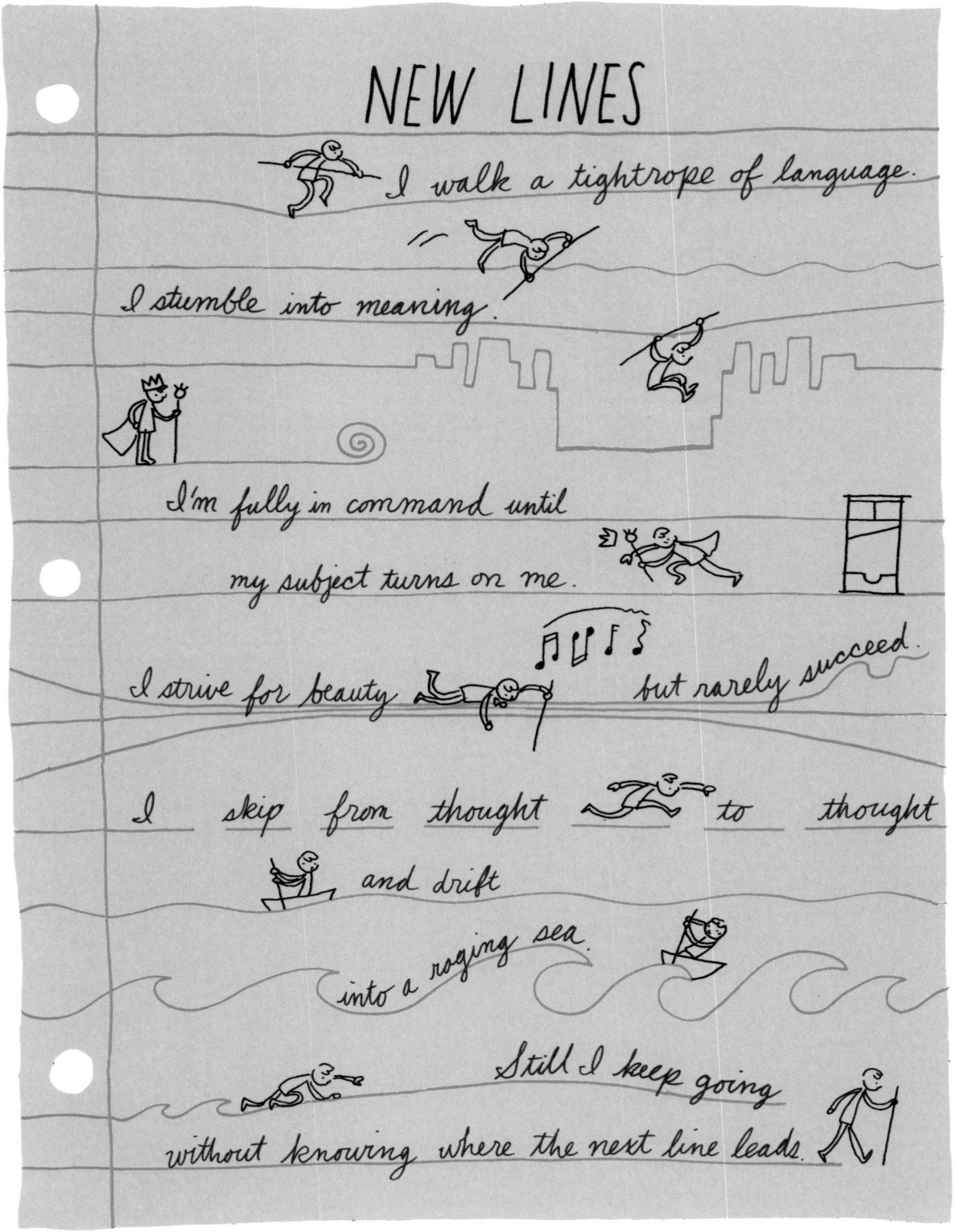
NEW LINES
I walk a tightrope of language.
I stumble into meaning.
I'm fully in command until
my subject turns on me.
I strive for beauty but rarely succeed.
I skip from thought to thought
and drift
into a raging sea.
Still I keep going
without knowing where the next line leads.

WHAT TO PUT IN YOUR NOTEBOOK

GOOD IDEAS 	BAD POEMS 	DARK SECRETS 	MISUNDERSTOOD SONG LYRICS 
POTENTIAL DOG NAMES 	RECIPES 	MAGIC SPELLS 	INTERESTING LEAVES 
WILD AMBITIONS 	HOPES 	FEARS 	USELESS INVENTIONS 
FEELINGS WITHOUT WORDS 	QUESTIONS 	MORE QUESTIONS 	YOURSELF. 

PERFECT

THIS IS THE PERFECT BOOK YOU WILL NEVER WRITE.

THIS IS THE PERFECT RACE YOU WILL NEVER RUN.

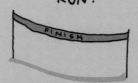

THIS IS THE PERFECT IDEA THAT WILL NEVER STRIKE.

THIS IS THE PERFECT PERSON YOU WILL NEVER BECOME.

THIS IS THE PERFECT PAINTING YOU WILL NEVER MAKE.

THIS IS THE PERFECT SONG YOU WILL NEVER HUM.

THIS IS THE PERFECT MOUNTAIN YOU WILL NEVER CLIMB.

THIS IS THE PERFECT CAKE YOU WILL NEVER BAKE.

THIS IS THE PERFECT SOLUTION YOU WILL NEVER FIND.

THIS IS PERFECTION:

IT DOESN'T EXIST.

TIME TO DESTROY PERFECT...

POOF

AND GET SOMETHING _DONE_.

I write
because I
must.

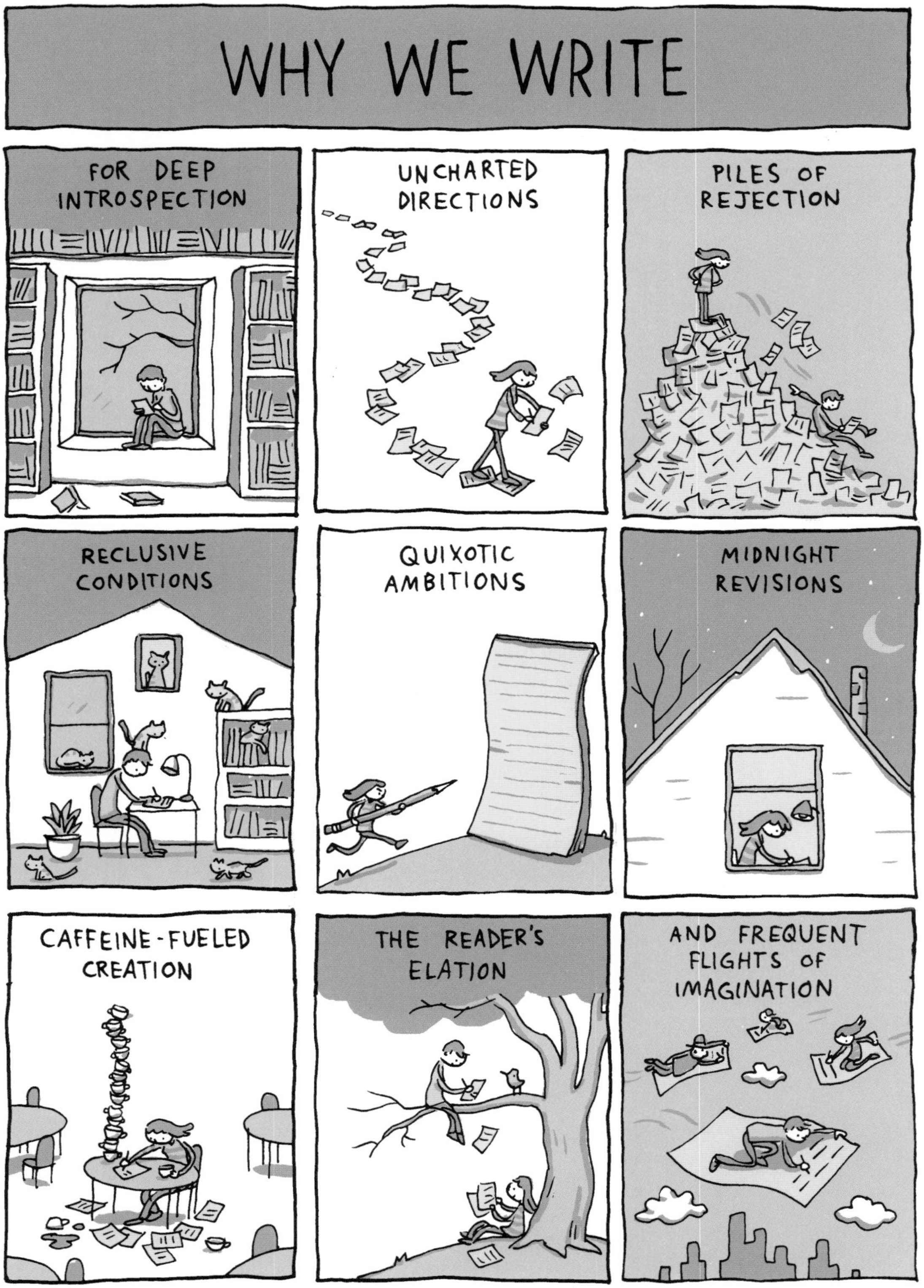
WHY WE WRITE
FOR DEEP INTROSPECTION
UNCHARTED DIRECTIONS
PILES OF REJECTION
RECLUSIVE CONDITIONS
QUIXOTIC AMBITIONS
MIDNIGHT REVISIONS
CAFFEINE-FUELED CREATION
THE READER'S ELATION
AND FREQUENT FLIGHTS OF IMAGINATION

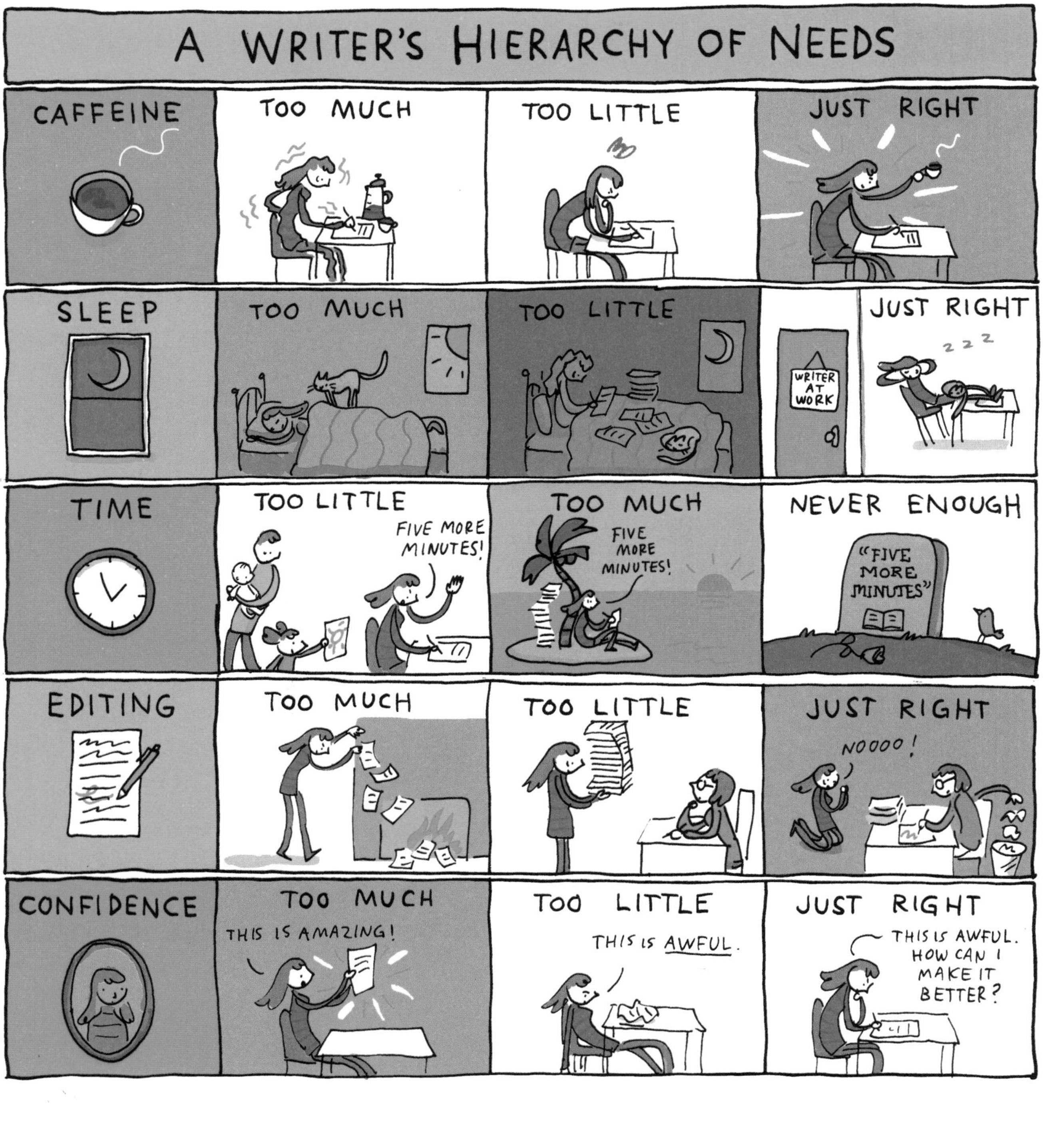
A WRITER'S HIERARCHY OF NEEDS
CAFFEINE
TOO MUCH
TOO LITTLE
JUST RIGHT
SLEEP
TOO MUCH
TOO LITTLE
WRITER AT WORK
JUST RIGHT
ZZZ
TIME
TOO LITTLE
FIVE MORE MINUTES!
TOO MUCH
FIVE MORE MINUTES!
NEVER ENOUGH
"FIVE MORE MINUTES"
EDITING
TOO MUCH
TOO LITTLE
JUST RIGHT
NOOOO!
CONFIDENCE
TOO MUCH
THIS IS AMAZING!
TOO LITTLE
THIS IS AWFUL.
JUST RIGHT
THIS IS AWFUL. HOW CAN I MAKE IT BETTER?

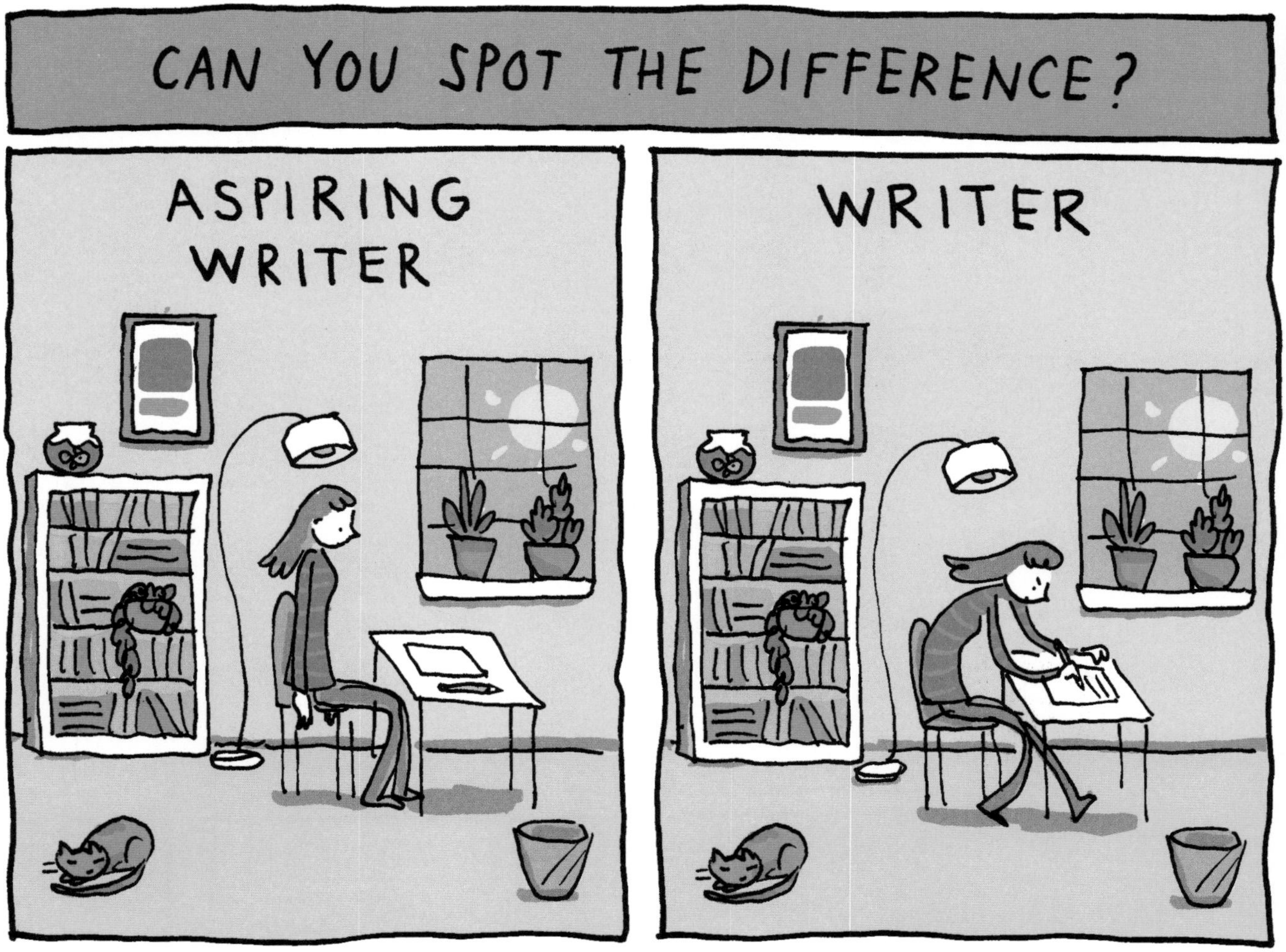
CAN YOU SPOT THE DIFFERENCE?
ASPIRING WRITER
WRITER

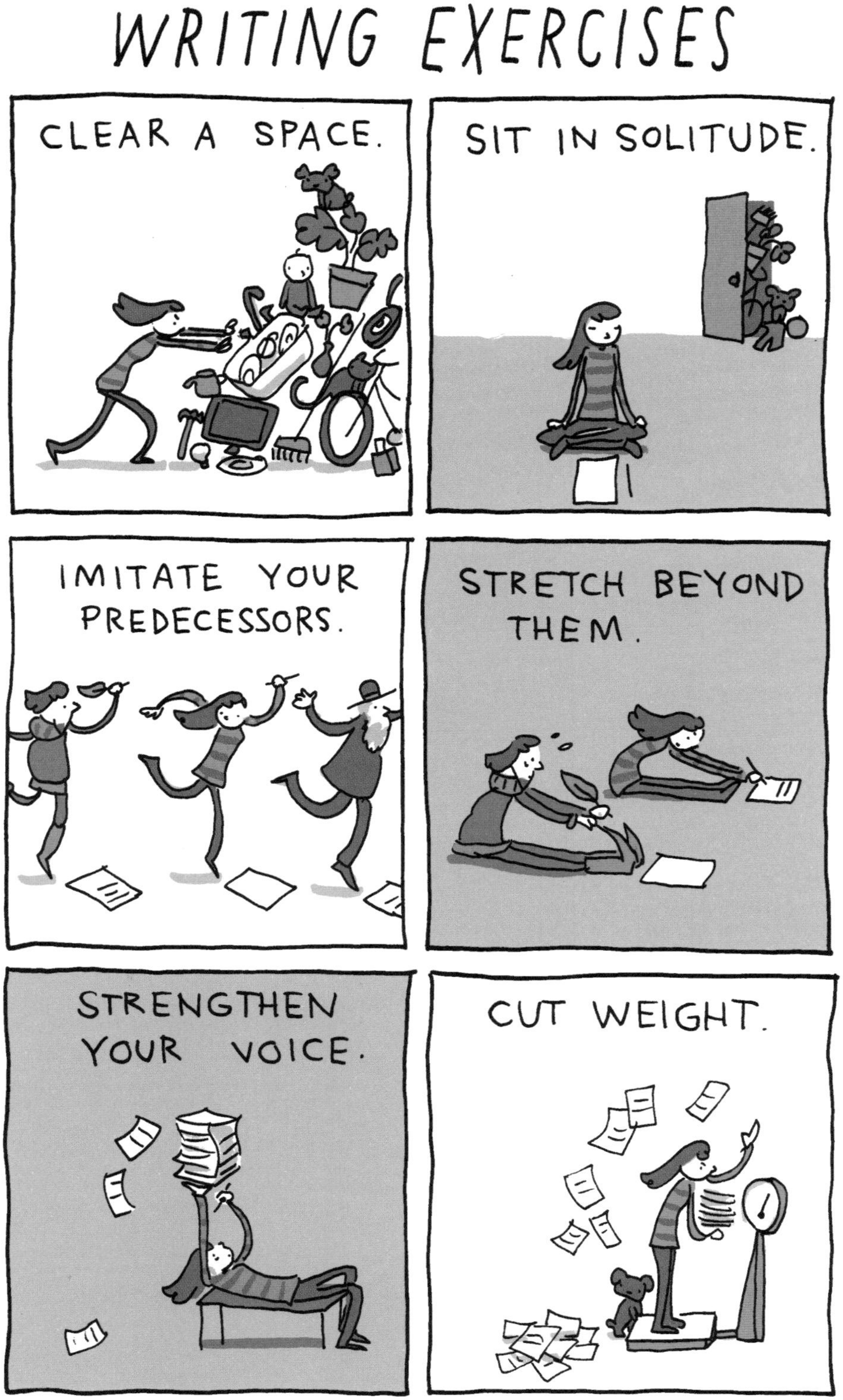
WRITING EXERCISES
CLEAR A SPACE.
SIT IN SOLITUDE.
IMITATE YOUR PREDECESSORS.
STRETCH BEYOND THEM.
STRENGTHEN YOUR VOICE.
CUT WEIGHT.

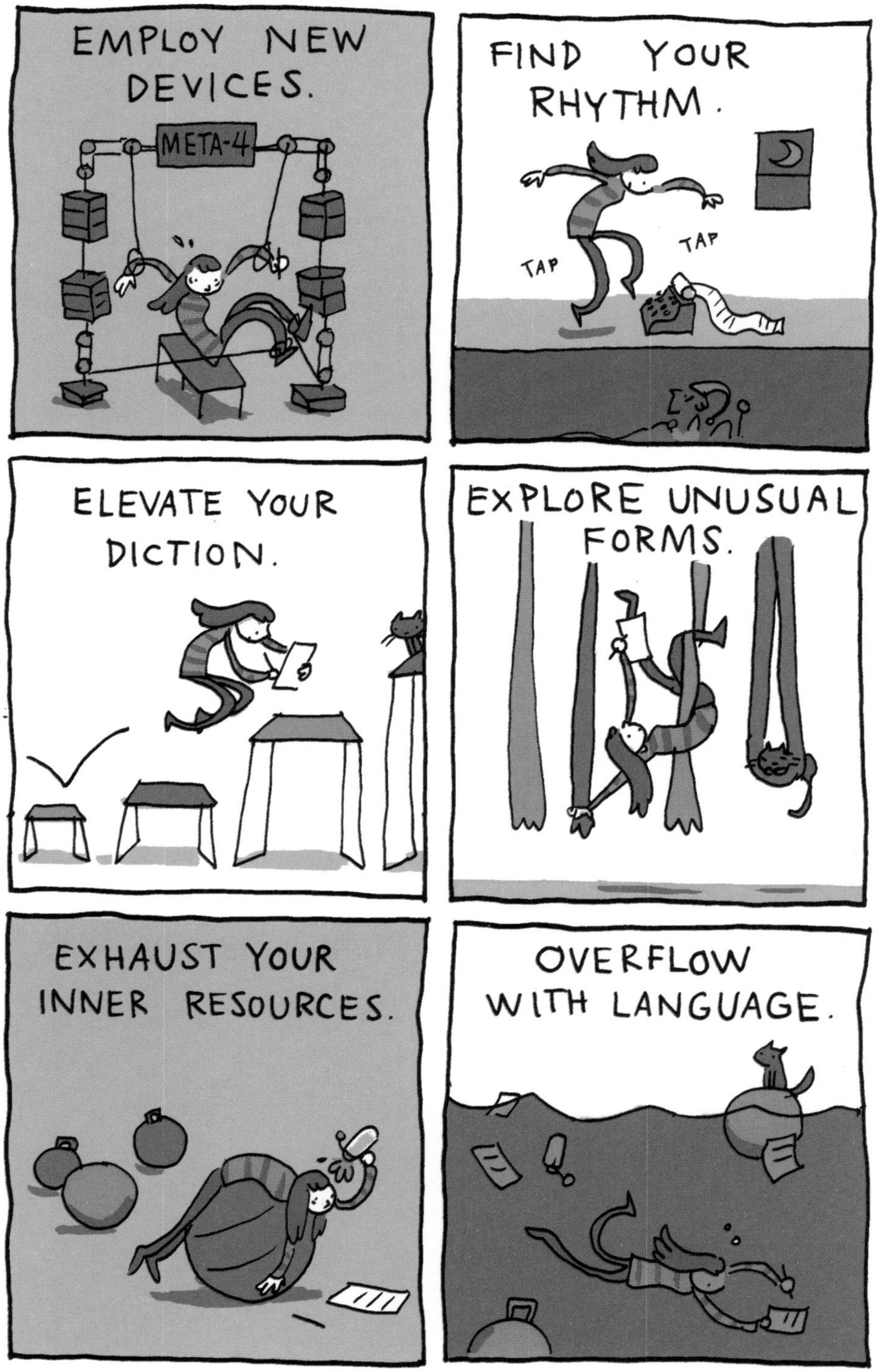
EMPLOY NEW DEVICES.
META-4
FIND YOUR RHYTHM.
TAP
TAP
ELEVATE YOUR DICTION.
EXPLORE UNUSUAL FORMS.
EXHAUST YOUR INNER RESOURCES.
OVERFLOW WITH LANGUAGE.

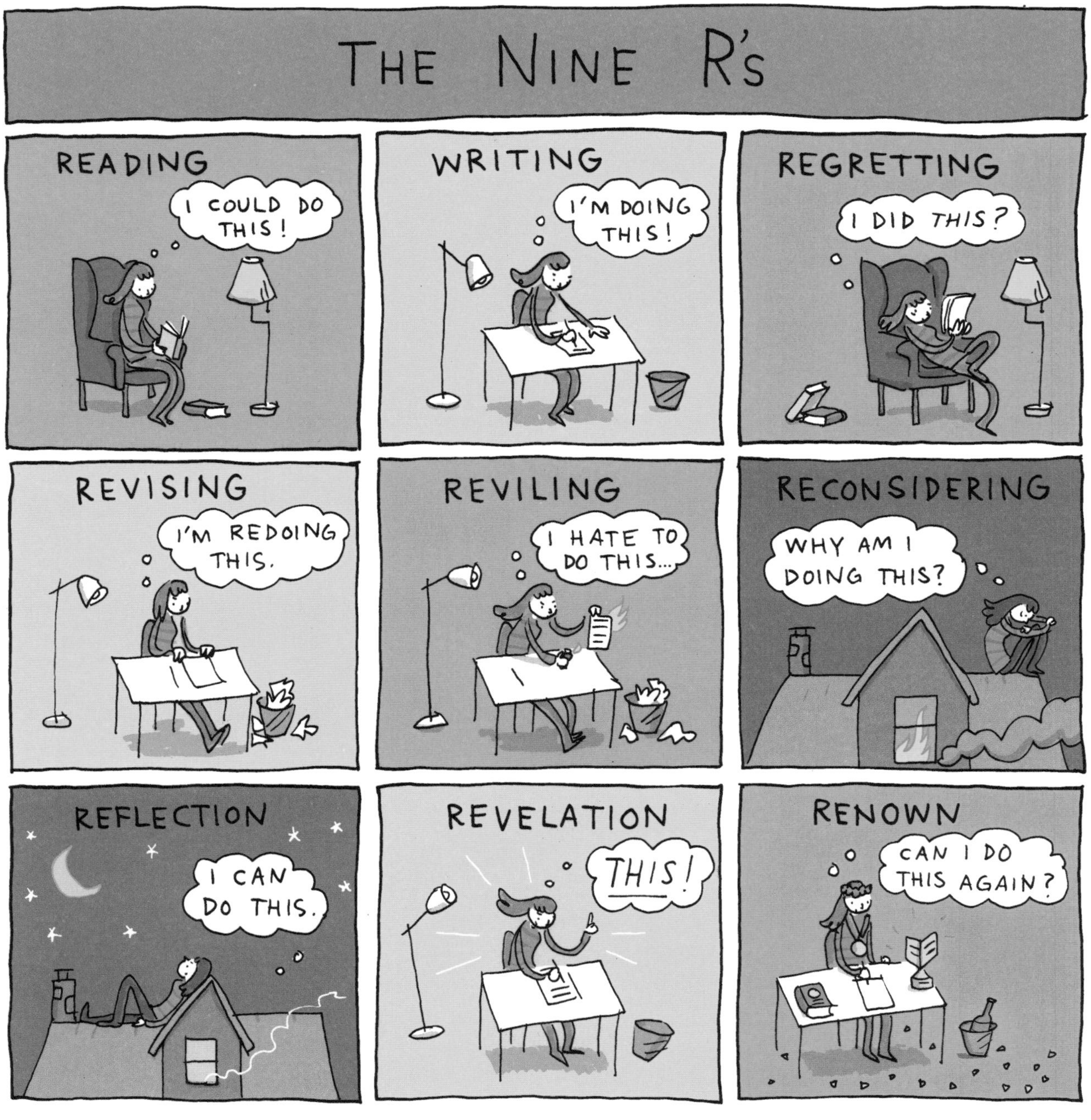
THE NINE R'S
READING
I COULD DO THIS!
WRITING
I'M DOING THIS!
REGRETTING
I DID THIS?
REVISING
I'M REDOING THIS.
REVILING
I HATE TO DO THIS...
RECONSIDERING
WHY AM I DOING THIS?
REFLECTION
I CAN DO THIS.
REVELATION
THIS!
RENOWN
CAN I DO THIS AGAIN?

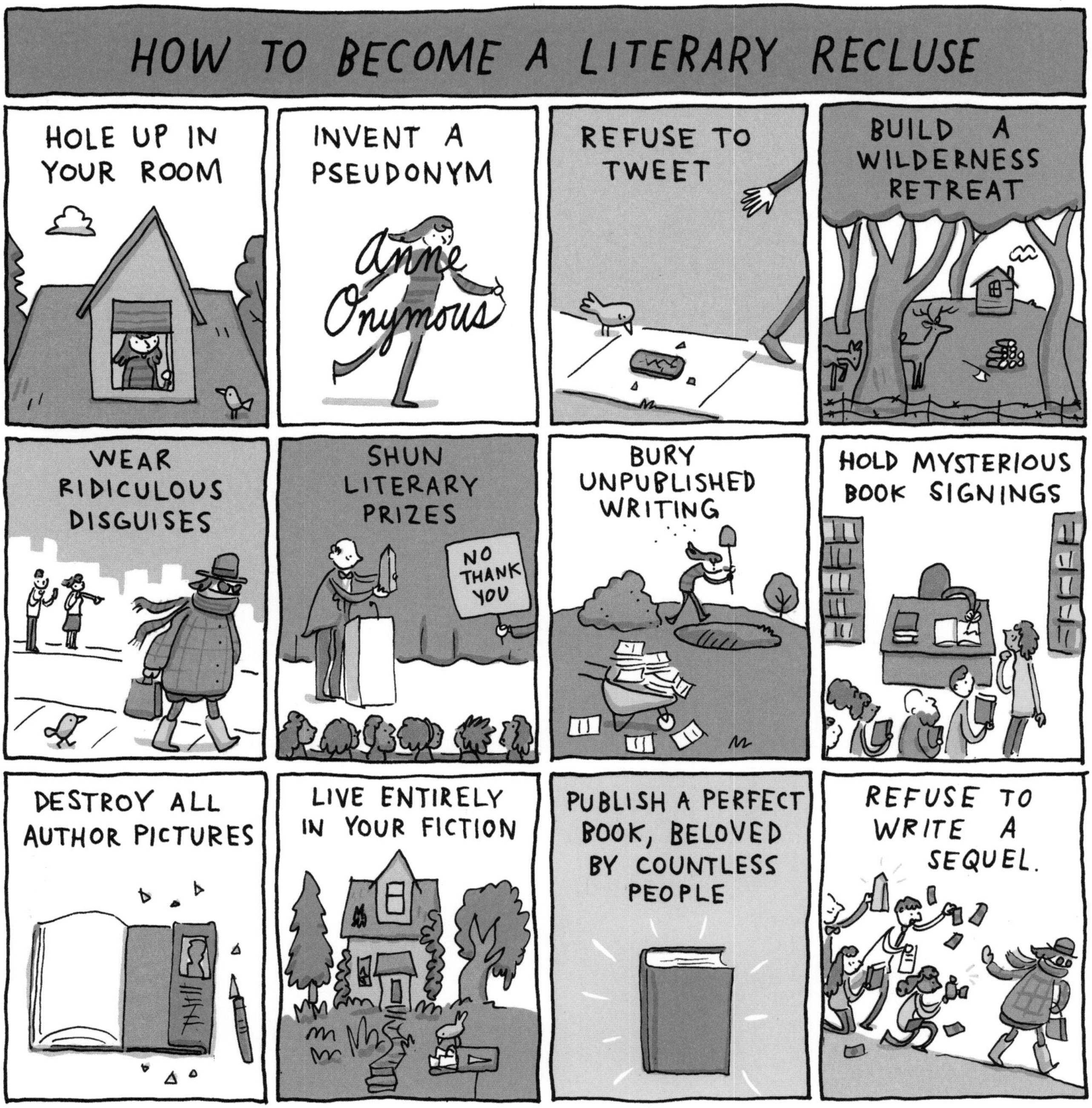
HOW TO BECOME A LITERARY RECLUSE
HOLE UP IN YOUR ROOM
INVENT A PSEUDONYM
Anne Onymous
REFUSE TO TWEET
BUILD A WILDERNESS RETREAT
WEAR RIDICULOUS DISGUISES
SHUN LITERARY PRIZES
NO THANK YOU
BURY UNPUBLISHED WRITING
HOLD MYSTERIOUS BOOK SIGNINGS
DESTROY ALL AUTHOR PICTURES
LIVE ENTIRELY IN YOUR FICTION
PUBLISH A PERFECT BOOK, BELOVED BY COUNTLESS PEOPLE
REFUSE TO WRITE A SEQUEL.

GREAT ASPIRATIONS

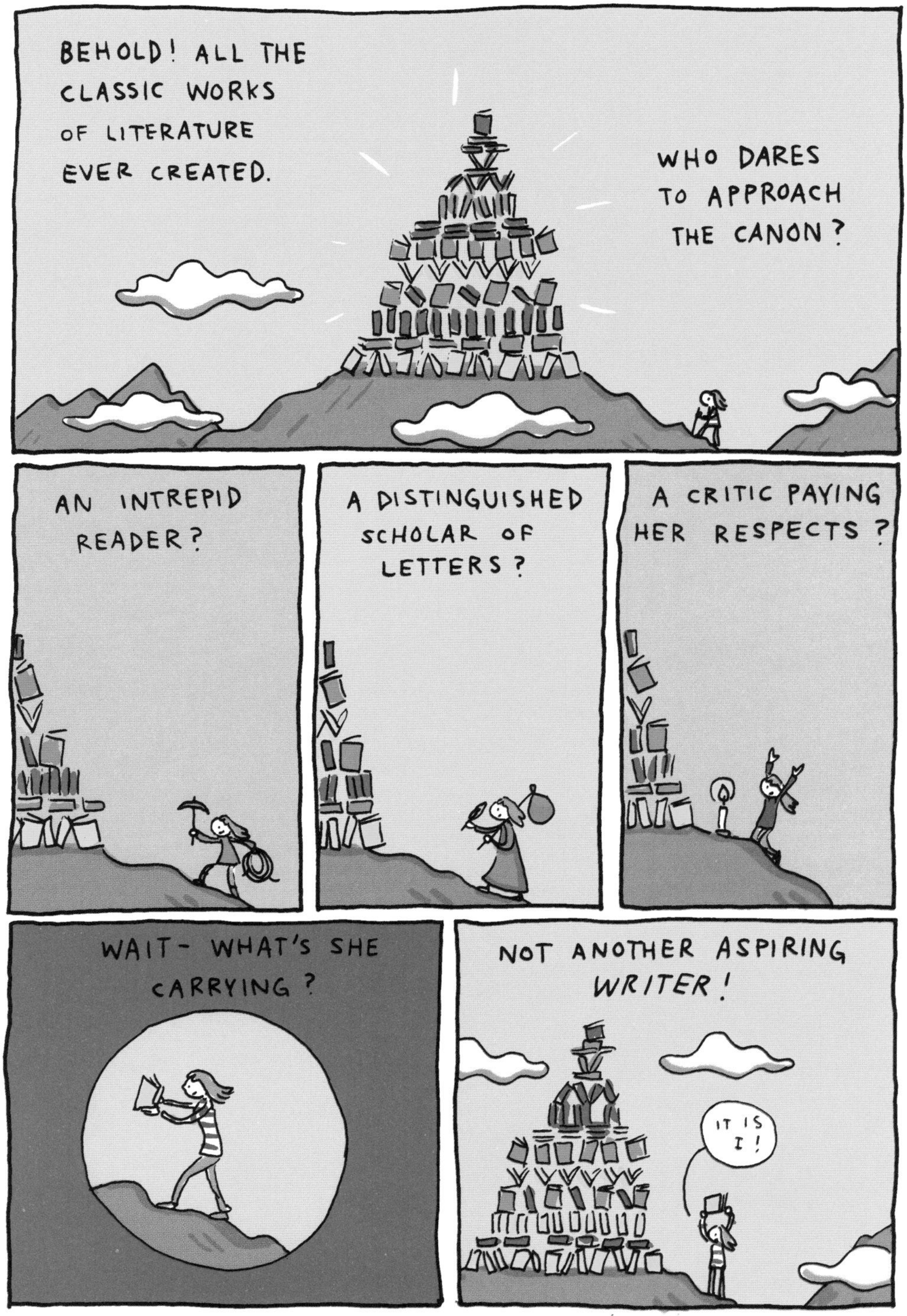
BEHOLD! ALL THE CLASSIC WORKS OF LITERATURE EVER CREATED.
WHO DARES TO APPROACH THE CANON?
AN INTREPID READER?
A DISTINGUISHED SCHOLAR OF LETTERS?
A CRITIC PAYING HER RESPECTS?
WAIT- WHAT'S SHE CARRYING?
NOT ANOTHER ASPIRING *WRITER*!
IT IS I!

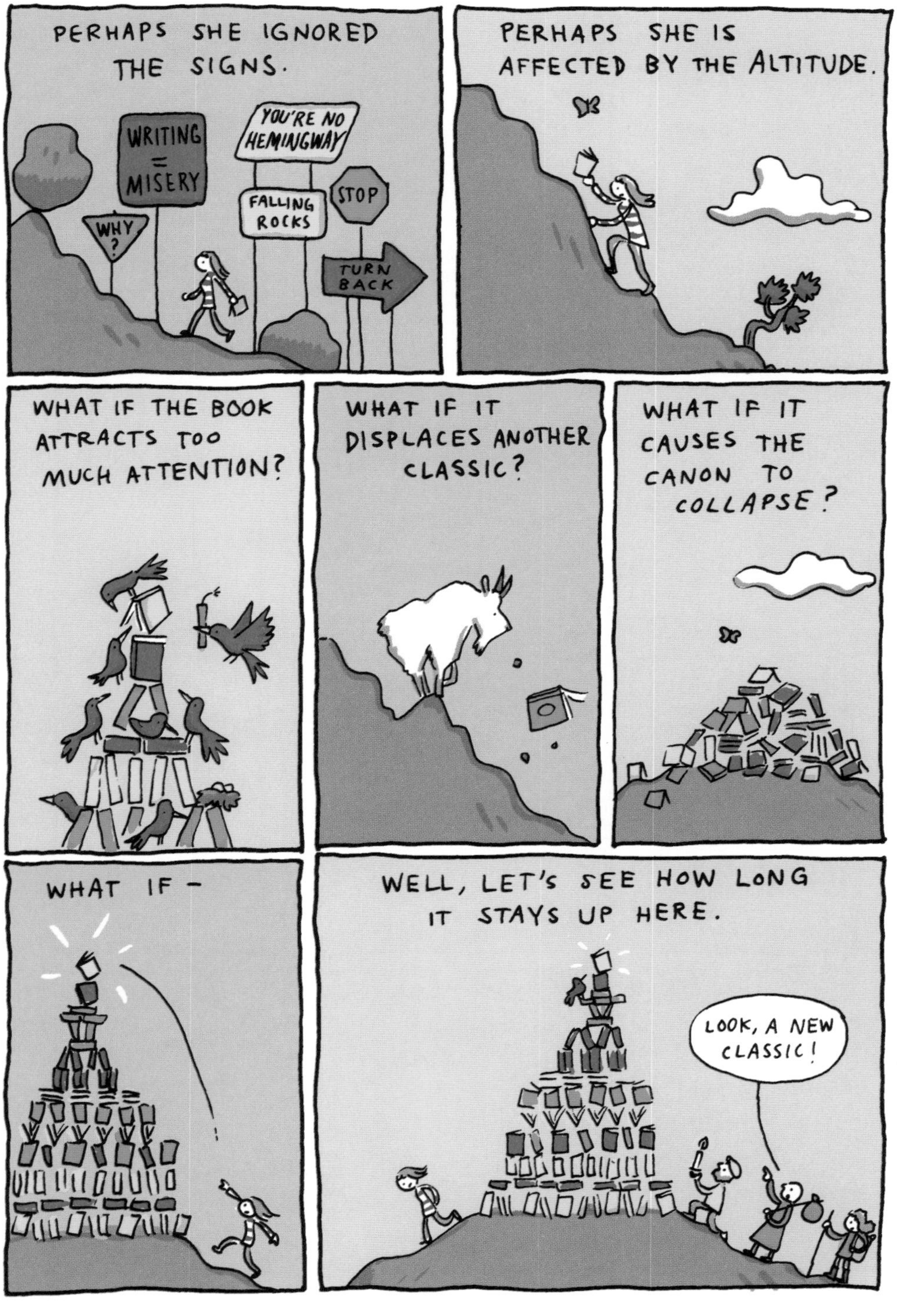
PERHAPS SHE IGNORED THE SIGNS.
WRITING = MISERY
WHY?
YOU'RE NO HEMINGWAY
FALLING ROCKS
STOP
TURN BACK
PERHAPS SHE IS AFFECTED BY THE ALTITUDE.
WHAT IF THE BOOK ATTRACTS TOO MUCH ATTENTION?
WHAT IF IT DISPLACES ANOTHER CLASSIC?
WHAT IF IT CAUSES THE CANON TO COLLAPSE?
WHAT IF -
WELL, LET'S SEE HOW LONG IT STAYS UP HERE.
LOOK, A NEW CLASSIC!

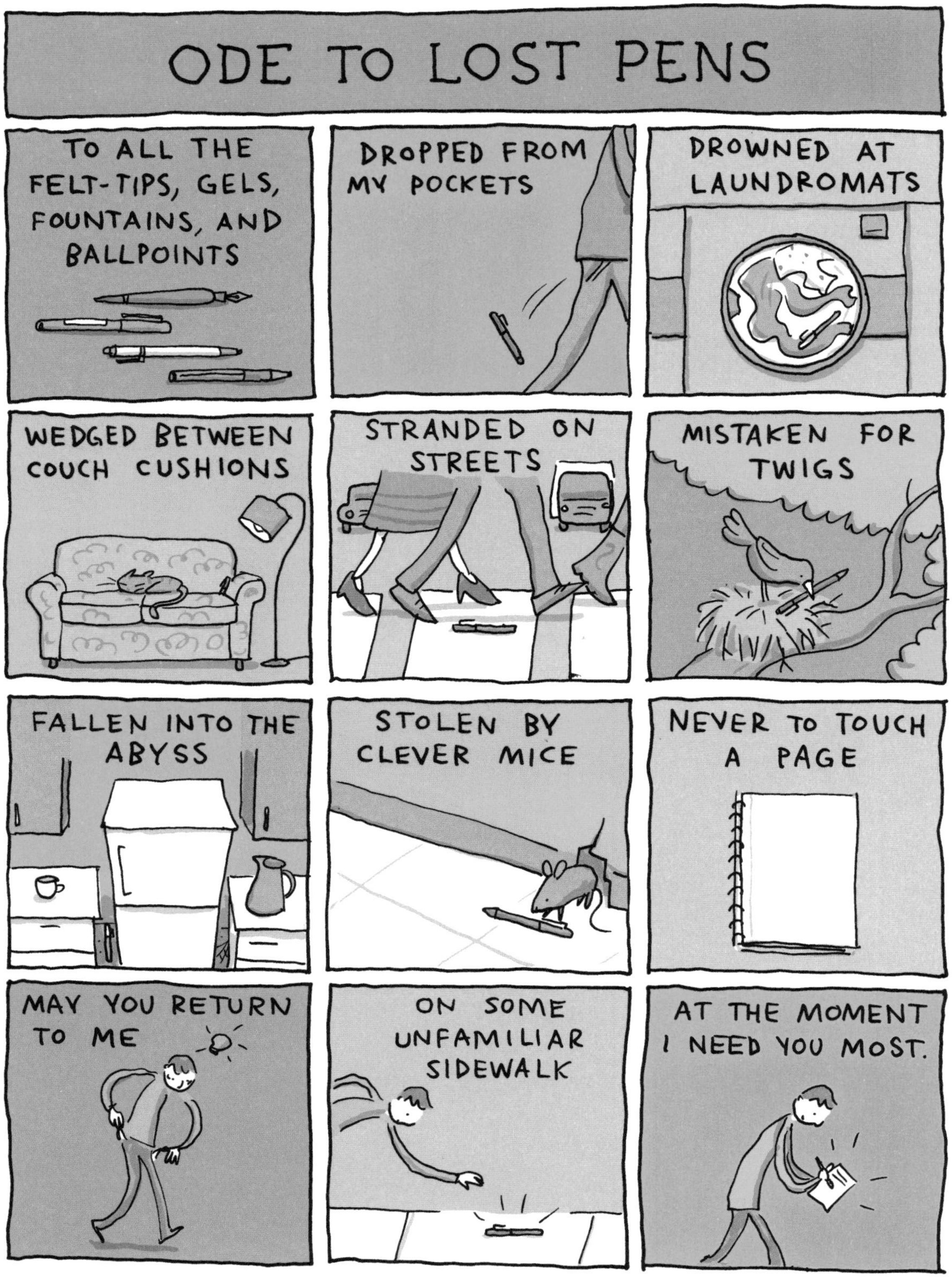
ODE TO LOST PENS
TO ALL THE FELT-TIPS, GELS, FOUNTAINS, AND BALLPOINTS
DROPPED FROM MY POCKETS
DROWNED AT LAUNDROMATS
WEDGED BETWEEN COUCH CUSHIONS
STRANDED ON STREETS
MISTAKEN FOR TWIGS
FALLEN INTO THE ABYSS
STOLEN BY CLEVER MICE
NEVER TO TOUCH A PAGE
MAY YOU RETURN TO ME
ON SOME UNFAMILIAR SIDEWALK
AT THE MOMENT I NEED YOU MOST.

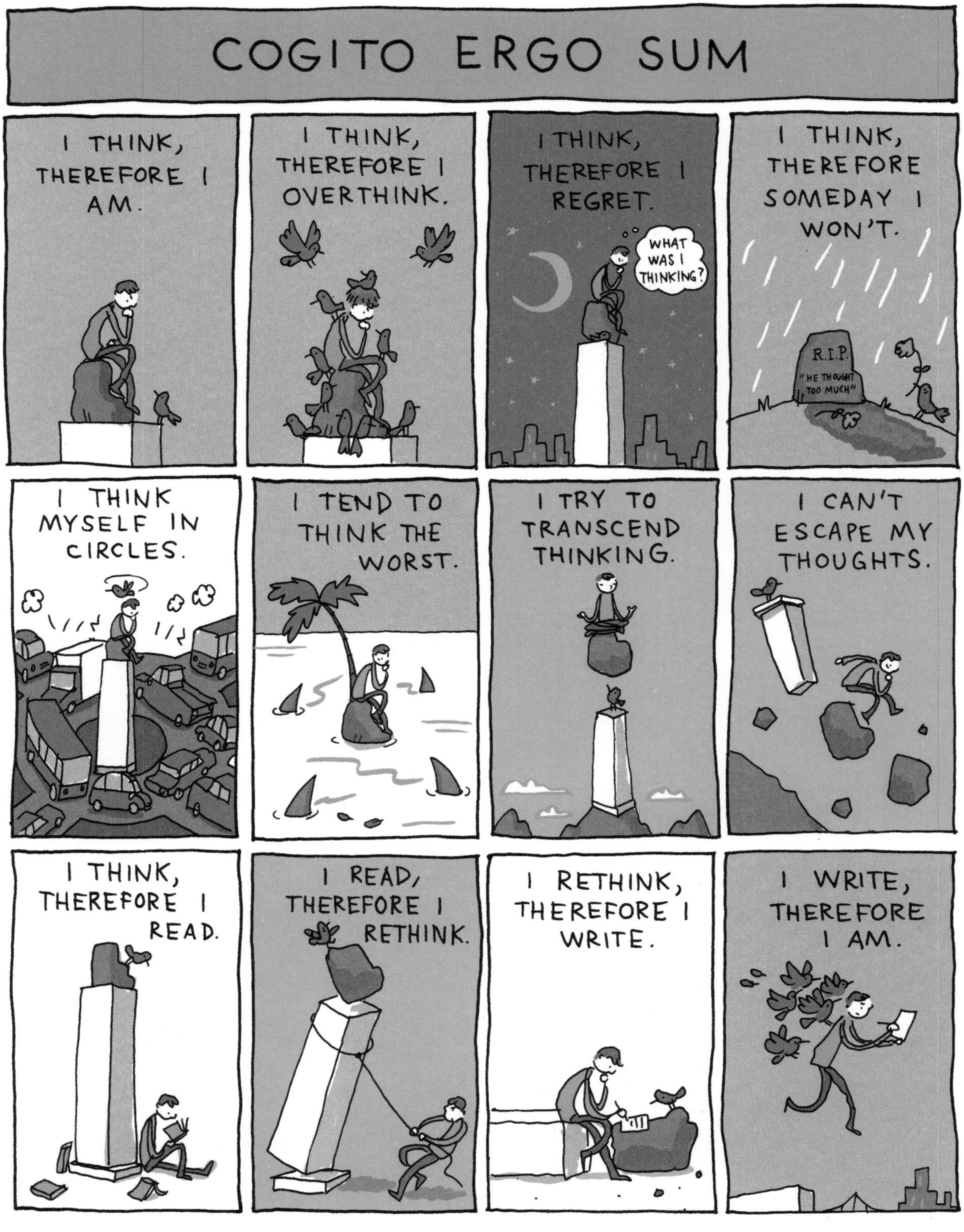

COGITO ERGO SUM
I THINK, THEREFORE I AM.
I THINK, THEREFORE I OVERTHINK.
I THINK, THEREFORE I REGRET.
WHAT WAS I THINKING?
I THINK, THEREFORE SOMEDAY I WON'T.
R.I.P.
"HE THOUGHT TOO MUCH"
I THINK MYSELF IN CIRCLES.
I TEND TO THINK THE WORST.
I TRY TO TRANSCEND THINKING.
I CAN'T ESCAPE MY THOUGHTS.
I THINK, THEREFORE I READ.
I READ, THEREFORE I RETHINK.
I RETHINK, THEREFORE I WRITE.
I WRITE, THEREFORE I AM.

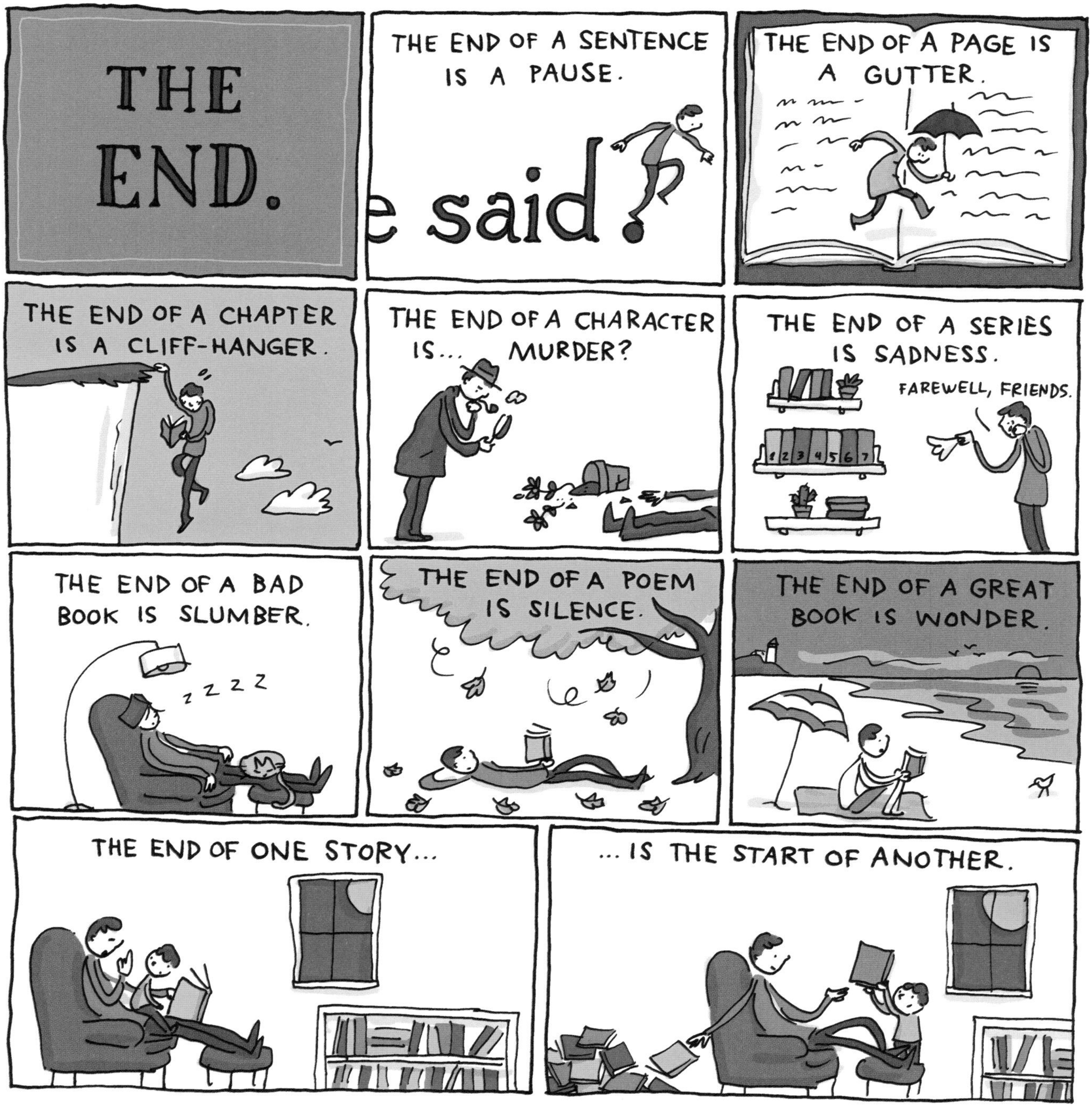
THE END.
THE END OF A SENTENCE IS A PAUSE.
e said?
THE END OF A PAGE IS A GUTTER.
THE END OF A CHAPTER IS A CLIFF-HANGER.
THE END OF A CHARACTER IS... MURDER?
THE END OF A SERIES IS SADNESS.
FAREWELL, FRIENDS.
THE END OF A BAD BOOK IS SLUMBER.
Z Z Z Z
THE END OF A POEM IS SILENCE.
THE END OF A GREAT BOOK IS WONDER.
THE END OF ONE STORY...
... IS THE START OF ANOTHER.

INDEX

earching for a miracle
or writer's block.

care about punctuation—a lot.

I will read the classics (someday).

I am writing The Great American Novel.

I carry a notebook with me at all times.

I write because I must.